DOING UP
A DUMP

DOING UP A DUMP

A DUMP

Barty Phillips

Macdonald

A **Macdonald** BOOK

© Barty Phillips 1985

First published in Great Britain in 1985
by Macdonald & Co (Publishers) Ltd
London & Sydney

A member of BPCC plc

British Library Cataloguing in Publication Data

Phillips. Barty
    Doing up a dump.
    1. Dwellings—Remodeling—Amateurs' manuals
    I. Title
    643'.7   TH4816

    ISBN 0-356-10829-5

Filmset by Flair plan Photo-typesetting Ltd.

Printed and bound in Milan, Italy by New Interlitho s.p.a.

Designed by Sarah Jackson

Illustrations by Raymond Turvey

Macdonald & Co (Publishers) Ltd
Maxwell House
74 Worship Street
London EC2A 2EN

Contents

Acknowledgements

The author and publishers would like to thank Susan Barnes, Sally Begg, Nick Colwill, Sarah Cowley, Philip and Jane Glynn, Colin Huntley, Diana Lipsey, Jane Priestman, Paul Priestman, Mark Prizeman and Lucy Voelcker for helping with suggestions, examples and/or allowing their homes to be photographed for this book.

Many thanks also to our photographer, Paul Beattie, and to the following companies who generously lent us photographs: Black & Decker, BP Aquaseal Ltd, British Home Stores plc, Cubestore, Futon Company, ICI Dulux, Interlübke, Laura Ashley, MFI Furniture Group plc, Moulinex Ltd, Ronseal, Sanderson Ltd, and The Sofa Bed Factory.

Introduction

One of the chief pleasures of leaving home for the first time is not just the freedom of keeping late hours and staying in bed until teatime if you feel like it, but the exotic freedom of living in an environment of your own making. If your idea of liberation is grubby sheets, bare light bulbs and beer stains on the carpet, this book is not for you. However, it will certainly come in useful when you've had enough of squalor. It's not a recipe for living in a dump so much as a challenge for turning a dump into a desirable place to come home to.

Doing up a Dump is mainly for young people, but I'd like to think that anyone with property (rented or owned) and on a limited budget could enjoy and make use of its ideas. The ideas themselves, of course, are only puffs of air. It's the way they are put together that will make them successful. They are all practicable, practical, cheerful, often stylish and usually fun. Many of them are far from new, but such ideas come into their own time and time again, especially with the present-day problems of finding cheap accommodation and coping on a meagre income.

I hope that students living in bedsits, first-time home buyers, young families and elderly folk moving into smaller houses will all find ideas and suggestions that will help them to make the best of a dingy bargain. All the ideas have been gleaned from personal experience, from the time I was a single parent and desperately trying to live on a pittance with three small children, and from friends of mine today, many of them young and unemployed, who somehow manage to live in surroundings which reflect their personality with style and dignity.

One of the most successful small apartments I know is furnished almost entirely from jumble sales, garage sales and the local DIY store, and is dominated by a jungle wall painting, executed by a friend with no experience whatever in 'art'. Colourful paper parrots, cut out of glossy magazines are moved about this jungle with a putty-type adhesive (see page 66). The same flat has a wall collage made from magazine cuttings and the ceiling is alive with little bird and fish mobiles picked up from charity shops. The result is a place of personality and charm, in spite of the concrete steps leading up to it and the battered entrance door.

Bricks and planks were a fashionable solution to the storage problem when I first set up home in the late fifties, and although various forms of inexpensive upright and bracket shelving are now available, anybody with a couple of old planks and access to a pile of bricks can build themselves a low bookcase practically free. Of course, modern materials and techniques open up possibilities not available in the past: coloured shelving can be bought in department stores; coloured grout for ceramic wall tiles can make a startling difference to a crummy kitchen or bathroom wall; durable, brightly coloured floor varnishes and paints can really make a worn floor look like new, and cost a great deal less than carpet.

All the ideas in this book can be adapted to different types and sizes of home and the varying attitudes and tastes of the people in them. Most of the photographs are of actual homes and the ideas shown really were cheap. As you'll see, it *is* possible to be very stylish on a tight budget.

I hope that readers will be entertained throughout this book and will find inspiration and encouragement to put their own ideas into practice as well as incorporating some of the ideas herein. One thing to remember about a dump, whether it's a basement, tenement or run-down Victorian terrace, is that you can let your imagination loose because you can't possibly make it worse than it is!

Overleaf: *Two small terraced houses show what a difference a little care and a spot of paint will do. The house with the blue door badly needs attention; the coving is beginning to fall off above the door and the window, the woodwork needs repairing and repainting and there's a concrete mess where the fence used to be. The house with the yellow door is painted, repointed, and the tiny well-tended garden gives it a sense of pride.*

1· First things first

Here you are. The proud occupant of your first home. It may be delapidated and dingy, it may be rented rather than owned, it may be full of the most hideous furniture, but for the time being at least it's all yours. True, now you come to look at it, it is probably a little smaller than you remember, and a little dingier and there doesn't seem to be much light coming into the kitchen; the carpets are horrible and how can you possibly conceal the dreadful wallpaper and where will all your books go? In fact, it's a dump.

Whether you expect to be in there for five years or a month, whether you've got money or not, this is going to be the heart of your life for a little while and the first thing to do is make it seem like home.

Cheer it up with flowers, put a big poster on the wall, introduce some bright colour in the shape of a red plastic vase or coffee maker,

This pile of old boxes and junk can hardly be anyone's dream of freedom and emancipation. Most of it will go straight into the skip.

old fashioned enamel tea and coffee tins with coloured lids, or a bright woven rug. You want warmth in colour and in texture.

Before you begin, you should discover your rights in relation to the property – whether you can change the paint colour or put up shelves without asking permission and how far the landlord has a say in what happens. Some landlords go out of their way to be helpful, and will even employ an architect who will offer choices of where the kitchen should be, what sort of window and door handles to have, even what colour of walls you would like. However, some landlords are horrible, feeling it their right to walk into your room whenever they want and threatening to turn you out if you don't behave as they say. Most fall between these two extremes, won't mind your doing things to the flat if they feel you are going to improve it and many will quite gladly increase your rent once you have upgraded it!

Getting permission

If you are the *freehold owner*, of course, you are free do more or less as you please in the way of altering, replacing or redecorating. (If you want to knock down a wall or put in a new lavatory or any other dramatic change, you should get an architect's advice and check with the local council about planning permission or building regulations.)

If you are a *council tenant* you should tread warily. It is demoralizing to be interrupted half way through some elaborate beautifying programme by the council decorators who have been ordered to paint every property the same shade of doggy brown. This has been known to happen, but many councils will be reasonable if you want to decorate your own place. Generally, the legal situation is like this: the landlord is obliged to maintain the structure of the building in good order, plus the services, such as plumbing and electricity, and shared areas such as hallways, forecourts, lifts and party walls. These costs, or most of them, are often passed back to the tenant in the form of a service charge.

If you own the *leasehold* of the place you may find there are certain restrictions. For instance, you may not be allowed to remove the landlord's hideous wall-to-wall carpet (in which case you'll have to try and conceal it with rugs or matting) or there may be restrictions on what sort of heater you are allowed to use. A number of leases do not allow paraffin heaters because of the danger of fire.

You will have to make sure that the inside is kept in good order, which means decorating every five years or so, maintaining the floorboards and surfaces and making sure the windows are repaired if they get broken. Provided you do this, keep the inside reasonably well cared for and you are not a nuisance, the landlord is only allowed to inspect the premises 'at a reasonable hour' and after giving you notice beforehand.

If you have a very lax landlord who has not seen that the water, gas and electricity supply installations are working properly, you can refer the matter to the public health authority or if necessary, get the work done and charge it to the landlord.

TENANT'S OBLIGATIONS

The Tenant will

(a) Pay the Rent at the times and in the manner specified.

(b) Pay for all gas and electric light and power which shall be consumed or supplied on or to the Property during the tenancy and the amount of the water rate charged in respect of the Property during the tenancy and the amount of all charges made for the use of the telephone (if any) on the Property during the tenancy or a proper proportion of the amount of such charges to be assessed according to the duration of the tenancy.

(c) Use the Property in a tenant-like manner.

(d) Not damage or injure the Property or make any alteration in or addition to it.

(e) Preserve the furniture and effects from being destroyed or damaged and not remove any of them from the Property.

(f) Yield up the Property at the end of the tenancy in the same clean state and condition as it was in at the beginning of the tenancy and make good pay for the repair of or replace all such items of the Fixtures Furniture and Effects as shall be broken lost damaged or destroyed during the tenancy (reasonable wear and tear and damage by fire excepted).

(g) Leave the Furniture and Effects at the end of the tenancy in the rooms or places in which they were at the beginning of the tenancy.

(h) Pay for the washing (including ironing or pressing) of all linen and for the washing and cleaning (including ironing or pressing) of all counterpanes blankets and curtains which shall have been soiled during the tenancy (the reasonable use thereof nevertheless to be allowed for).

(i) Permit the Landlord or the Landlord's agents at reasonable hours in the daytime to enter the Property to view the state and condition thereof and of the Fixtures Furniture and Effects.

(j) Not assign underlet charge or part with possession of the Property without the previous consent in writing of the Landlord.

(k) Not carry on on the Property any profession trade or business or let apartments or receive paying guests on the Property or place or exhibit any notice-board or notice on the Property or use the Property for any other purpose than that of a strictly private residence.

(l) Not do or suffer to be done on the Property anything which may be or become a nuisance or annoyance to the Landlord or the tenants or occupiers of any adjoining premises or which may vitiate any insurance of the property against fire or otherwise or increase the ordinary premium for such insurance.

(m) Permit the Landlord or the Landlord's agents at reasonable hours in the daytime within the last twenty-eight days of the tenancy to enter and view the Property with prospective tenants.

LANDLORD'S OBLIGATIONS

The Landlord agrees with the Tenant as follows:—

(1) To pay and indemnify the Tenant against all rates taxes assessments and outgoings in respect of the Property (except the water rate and except charges for the supply of gas or electric light and power or the use of any telephone).

(2) That the Tenant paying the Rent and performing the agreements on the part of the Tenant may quietly possess and enjoy the Property during the tenancy without any lawful interruption from the Landlord or any person claiming under or in trust for that party.

(3) To return to the Tenant any rent payable for any period while the Property is rendered uninhabitable by fire the amount in case of dispute to be settled by arbitration.

The obligations of tenant and landlord are clearly stated in most tenancy agreements. The clauses shown here apply to rented accommodation.

Shades of green and porridge are used here to create a calm atmosphere emphasized by the plants. The sheer curtains at the window help to contribute to the cool, quiet underwater feeling. Most of the effect is produced by clever use of paint and the careful placing of the accessories: the lamps, the cushions and the dragonflies above the fireplace are echoed on the screen.

Whatever the circumstances, if you want to do anything other than decorating, you should get approval from your landlord. Write him a friendly letter telling him what you want to do and include details of the work and any drawings required. If it's a big alteration, planning permission or by-law approval may be needed from the local authority and you should apply in writing enclosing specifications and drawings.

You will have to apply to the landlord if you want to remove a partition or if you want to knock a hole through an outside wall for such reasons as rewiring, installing central heating, fitting an extra bathroom or lavatory, or knocking two rooms into one. All of these are counted as structural alterations.

You are usually allowed to change the sanitary fittings (but not to

Shades of green and porridge are used here to create a calm atmosphere emphasized by the plants. The sheer curtains at the window help to contribute to the cool, quiet underwater feeling. Most of the effect is produced by clever use of paint and the careful placing of the accessories: the lamps, the cushions and the dragonflies above the fireplace are echoed on the screen.

add extra ones) and improve and redecorate the plasterwork, floor tiles and wall tiles. The landlord usually has no control over the colour or the texture of any fittings or surfaces that you choose, but it may be wise to check with him first.

You may be able to change the door and window handles, sand or replace floorboards and add built-in furniture, but you may not remove existing built-in furniture (or any furniture which you have built in) without the landlord's consent. So it's sensible to put in freestanding furniture if you think you will want to take it with you when you go.

You can replace kitchen fittings during the term of the lease, but must put back the landlord's own fittings when you leave, or pay compensation for them if your own additions are not an improvement. So if you do remove the landlord's fittings, make sure you put them in a safe place and remember where they are. The tenant can improve or replace the glass in the windows and the floor and wall tiles.

Whether you are the owner or a tenant the chances are you don't have much spare cash. You will either be stretched financially by your mortgage or by your rent, or you may be on the dole. Don't be disheartened. This book is about creating comfort cheaply out of poor basic material. There are inexpensive ways of concealing ugly corners, badly shaped rooms, poky staircases and bad surfaces, ways of making dark rooms lighter and of turning a little hole of a place into something pleasant.

Priorities

The shorter the time you intend to stay in the place, the less you will want to spend. Really, you have a choice of two techniques: the conceal, cover-up and pretend technique for horrible little condemned and hard-to-let properties you hope you won't be in for long, and the scrape-down, fill-in, paint-up and furnish-by-degrees technique for a place which is to be yours for some years.

If you really are only staying for a month, then you will obviously want to invest in the short term and the cheap. Flowers have an extraordinary ability to change the mood of a place for the better. Plastic flowers can be used to good effect and won't fade, though may need washing occasionally. Postcards and posters can be arranged to cover most of the walls; cushions are cheaper than chairs.

If you are staying longer, even if only a year, there are fascinating possibilities which won't cost a bomb. I made loose covers for a three-piece suite in a flat I had no intention of being in for more than a year. I enjoyed making them, enjoyed sitting in them and didn't mind leaving them behind to cover the horrible, cow-pat brown chairs for the next tenant since they definitely would never have fitted any chairs I might buy myself later.

But do some sums; work out how much money you actually have to spend and what really has to be done first before you start on the luxuries. If there are two or more of you in this together get it absolutely straight between you who is financially responsible for what and make sure that each person will really be able to contribute what they say they will.

The more jobs you can do yourself, the cheaper the scheme will be. Painting and papering are only difficult if the ceilings are very high or you have six layers of old wallpaper and paint to scrape off before you can begin. One of the advantages of an attic is that the ceiling is so low you can reach it without steps or a ladder. Cushions and curtains are easily made if you have a sewing machine and a little experience; roller blinds can be made pretty cheaply with a kit, and paint can transform fridges, floors, walls, furniture and storage canisters.

Make one room, or one corner of it if you only have the one room, habitable and pleasant immediately so you can escape there and put your feet up when the chaos elsewhere becomes intolerable. If you're on the longer-than-six-months kick, plan your works and do the basic stuff first. No amount of prettying up will conceal the smell of a damp wall or the sight of peeling wallpaper or the fact that there's no cupboard to put things in. So the first thing is to clear and clean the basic shell as thoroughly as you can. Most places are filthy when you move into them so get lots of cleaner, plenty of cloths, a large bucket and scrubbing brush and really get down to it. Then you can have a good look at the bare bones of your home.

A ready-furnished place is usually a disadvantage. The sort of furniture landlords put into furnished rooms is generally what they don't want themselves or the cheapest old tat they can lay their hands on at auctions: tables whose legs stick out at awkward angles, enormous wardrobes, drawers that won't open and then won't close, uncomfortable chairs and minutely narrow beds. Pile them all up to one side, or out in the hall if you can, while you look at the space and decide what to do with it.

Repair as best you can bad plasterwork, splintery wood, dangerous stairs and light fittings and prepare the surface for whatever you intend to cover it with. Walls really do need washing or even scraping if the paint is to adhere and it is discouraging to see paint peel off which you only put there a week ago. Move the furniture right out of the way when you paint. It's hopelessly difficult to try and paint behind the shelves on a wall and much less trouble in the long run to move the shelves first and put them back afterwards.

Whatever you do – short term, long term, slapdash, dramatic or discreet, you can do it cheaply with ingenuity, imagination and an acquisitive attitude.

2·Finding the cash

If the improvements you plan to make are substantial rather than cheap and cheerful, don't go rushing into the bank to borrow money before you know exactly how much you will need. Raising cash calls for as much planning as the work itself. If you don't know how much you want and why, you could easily find yourself paying too much for an unsuitable loan. If you are clever and follow this book carefully, you might not need to borrow money at all.

However, even if you are fairly handy, it takes ages to decorate thoroughly and well, especially if there's a lot of repair or cleaning up work to be done first. You may in the long run find it more satisfactory to call in somebody local to do some of the work rather than begin a long and complicated job which you can only work on at weekends. Plastering is difficult, messy and tiring. Dry rot and woodworm should be treated by professionals. Laying floors, stripping paint, renewing woodwork, painting and wallpapering can all be done by you and save money, but you may not have the time.

If you do decide to get help, get an estimate or better still, ask two or three builders for estimates and compare their offers. For small jobs which are likely to start at once and not take longer than a few weeks, the builder should be asked to keep his prices firm and not to ask for increases due to fluctuations in the cost of labour and materials. The advantage of having estimates before work starts is that you can calculate exactly what you can afford and leave out certain items rather than have the frustration of starting something you can't finish.

Getting a loan

Before you commit yourself to borrowing anything do some basic budgeting of your weekly or monthly incomings: earnings, social security, grant or allowance. Deduct your outgoings for bills, food, travel and so on, and what you have left is what you can spend. Almost certainly, it won't be much, so be realistic in deciding what you can achieve. If you intend to do most of the decorating yourself with help and rollers from friends, you can do it very cheaply indeed.

How do you compare the cost of a three-year loan from a bank with

---

BETTER BUILDERS LTD   46 New Road, Puddletown
Telephone: 178 1234

Specification of works to 1st floor, 23 Nonesuch Road, Puddletown
for Miss Brown.

1. Cut out and replace bathroom ceiling	130
2. Overhaul bedroom window with new sash cords & beading	35
3. Cut out and renew kitchen windowsill. Fix closed left-hand sash and improve right-hand sash.	45
4. Reglaze skylight	35
Total works sum	245

This estimate remains open for acceptance for 30 days.
We will require 50% of total works amount in advance; remainder
payable on completion.

This is a fairly standard builder's estimate for some straightforward work. If you prefer, materials and labour may be itemized separately.

a five-year loan from a finance house? Finance house loans are usually spread over a longer period and cost less in monthly repayments and more in the long run. Make sure you have any scheme explained clearly to you and go to more than one source of money before you make up your mind which to take. Borrowing for ten years and paying off within five could cost you more than borrowing for five years in the first place. Work out the minimum period during which you can afford to repay a loan as it may be worth taking on high repayments.

For most people there are four choices: building societies, banks, finance houses and insurance companies.

Building societies usually charge lower rates of interest than banks and finance companies and the repayment period may be very long. If you already have a building society savings account, you should start there.

Banks lend on a personal basis. The friendlier you are with your bank manager, the more likely he is to lend you money. Also bank managers usually appreciate it if you go with a good plan and something down on paper which they will be impressed by. Ask for a lower rate of interest than the one you are offered. Bank managers are often prepared to bargain, which is an advantage, though their repayment time is usually short – about three years – which may be a disadvantage.

Finance houses provide money for most hire purchase and instal-

Left: *A skip is a sign that a house is being cared for. There's always the vague hope that there may be something worthwhile to salvage.*

Some problems, such as serious damp, may require professional attention. In this case it has completely altered the possibilities in a small basement.

ment credit agreements. They also lend lump sums, often making their services known through newspaper advertisements, or by sending circulars through your letterbox. They are easy to deal with, lend over long periods and to people who can't borrow elsewhere, but their rates of interest are usually higher. As a rule, go to them last.

Insurance companies normally only lend to people who have policies to offer as security and these loans may be attractive because of the low rates of interest. By taking out this sort of loan you may be affecting your insurance protection and if you have a family, *their* insurance protection, so check thoroughly before agreeing to such a loan.

When working out the sum you want to borrow, remember that you will have to pay interest on it and must include it in your sums. It's always more than you think. You can normally get tax relief on the interest paid on money borrowed for home improvements. The scale of the relief will depend on the extent of the project, but major structural improvements should qualify for relief on the whole interest.

Your local tax office and the lending institution should be consulted early on about the status of the interest payments for tax purposes. If you are a standard rate taxpayer and have enough taxable income to absorb the relief, you may be able to make substantial tax savings on the interest you pay. Allow for this when budgeting, but remember that tax laws governing relief are subject to frequent changes.

Handing over the cash

Payments to a builder or decorator should be made at regular intervals, either weekly or monthly. You should pay promptly to make sure the builder continues to be well disposed and efficient on your behalf. Some will want to be paid in cash every Friday, so arrange to have the cash ready. Very few painters are secretly interior decorators at heart, and most will be much happier if you know what you want and just tell them what it is, without asking their advice all the time. You can either buy the materials yourself or the builder will get them at a trade discount. Do not ask the decorators to do odd little favours such as, 'Could you just put up the bathroom cupboard' or 'Could you just fix this mirror?' Such tiny items will all be added to the bill and can cost quite a lot extra as well as annoying the workmen.

Agree the working hours, say from 8 a.m. to 5 p.m. with an hour's break for lunch, five days a week. These precautions may seem unnecessary and even a bit embarrassing between reasonable people, but your priorities and those of the builders are not the same and misunderstandings are easy to achieve. Where expensive work is concerned it is well to reach a firm agreement rather than find yourself not on speaking terms half way through the job.

Finally, if you hire someone whose work you know is good, make sure he's going to come and do the job himself and not send a subcontractor instead.

First floor
23 Nonesuch Road
Puddletown

14 May

Better Builders Ltd
46 New Road
Puddletown

Dear Mr Smith

This letter confirms my acceptance of your estimate for the works to be done to my flat.

As agreed by telephone, work will start on Monday, 5 June and be completed no later than Friday, 9 June.

The working hours will be 8 a.m. to 5 p.m. with one hour for lunch and two ten-minute tea-breaks.

All debris and dirt caused by the building work will be removed by you daily.

You will take all reasonable care to avoid damage to the flat and fittings, but should damage occur, an agreed sum will be deducted from the final payment.

I enclose herewith the first payment for the work, the balance to be paid when everything has been satisfactorily completed.

Yours sincerely

J. Brown.

Jane Brown

Here is a sample letter of agreement that covers the main points most likely to cause difficulty or misunderstanding. Although not legally binding, it makes responsibilities and expectations quite clear.

3· The shell

Some people enjoy painting and putting up wallpaper; others haven't the patience for it. Applying one coat of paint is OK, but having to do several is boring. Certainly there's no point at all in putting effort into a condemned building, but given that the place has some potential, it pays to prepare the ground. Otherwise you're simply doing the equivalent of exquisitely embroidering an old rag. Preparation is important, no matter how tedious. Here are the most likely problems and some of the things that can be done about them.

Damp

You may find dampness inside cupboards, creeping up walls or in the corner of the ceiling. I found a very damp wall behind the piano after the instrument had been in the same place for years. It was discovered that the rainwater gutter had been blocked with leaves and was overflowing down the outside wall which was covered in a green mould. Inside, the wallpaper was beginning to blister and peel away. In a situation like this, it is not just the wallpaper which is affected. Eventually the damp will encourage fungus and you will get the dreaded dry rot or wet rot which can eat its way through joists and beams at high speed and cost an arm and a leg to cure, besides smelling of decay.

There are several possible causes of damp: a faulty damp proof course, porous brickwork, neglected pointing, leaking gutters or down pipes, defective flashings on the roof or missing roof tiles. You should identify the cause or ask a builder to do so and get it dealt with as soon as you can. Then you can treat the wall inside, using one of the various water repellent treatments that you can find at builders' merchants. Some of them can be applied even while the walls are still damp.

Ceilings and walls

Nearly all houses 'move' a bit as they settle in their foundations and as the ground they are built on moves with changes in weather. While this is happening, cracks sometimes appear in the walls and

The sorry sight above is horrible to live with since it looks and smells awful, causes dampness in the house and rot in the fabric of the building.

After it had been treated, the little semi-basement area could be used with some pleasure.

often where the wall meets the ceiling. You'll never get rid of these but you can hide them behind a textured paper or ceiling cove. You can buy ready-made coving which can be cut with a fine tooth saw and stuck on with a special adhesive supplied by the makers. You can paint the cove afterwards.

Small cracks in the walls can usually be mended with cellulose filler. Wide cracks may need patching with scrim mesh (from DIY shops) and lining paper.

If the plaster has loosened near the fireplace or where there has been a damp problem, the loose bits should be lifted out with a broad knife and repairs made with thistle plaster, which is very hard. Do the deed quickly or the plaster will dry before you apply it.

Small holes in a plaster ceiling can be mended with cellulose filler or plaster. A really big hole which looks as though a broom has been poked through it should be plugged with stiff, dampened paper (like *papier mâché*) which will provide something for the new plaster to adhere to. A badly cracked or damaged ceiling should be watched carefully and if it shows signs of collapsing – large chunks falling off, for instance – you will have to get the whole thing replastered. If you're worried, get your landlord or a builder to look at it.

Whitewash is hardly ever used now, but it used to be the standard cheap paint finish for many ceilings and you may still find whitewashed ceilings in old properties. Unfortunately, it is incredibly difficult to remove, powdering away by degrees and falling into your eyes as you scrape it. The only satisfactory way to get rid of it is

Repairing plaster
1   Fill the hole with paper, roughly level with the surrounding plaster.
2   Use cellulose filler or plaster to cover the paper and fill the hole, spreading it evenly with a trowel.
3   Using a dampened paintbrush, smooth out the plaster so it is level with the rest of the ceiling. Leave it to dry completely before painting.

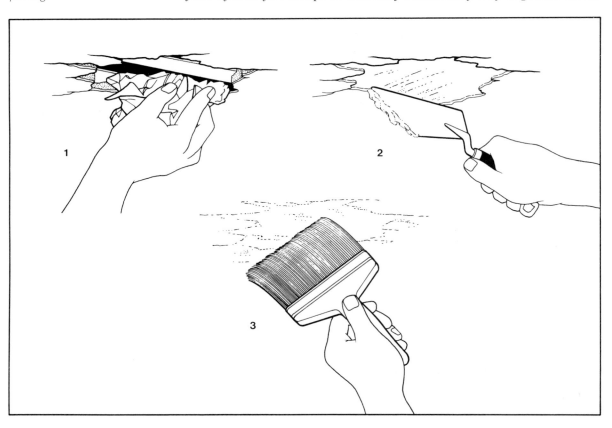

to brush patiently with a broom until it's all removed. Never use it again, but go for washable emulsion paints (vinyl or acrylic).

Floorboards

Among the cheapest and nicest-looking floors are sanded and sealed boards. They are often made of pine and become a lovely rich yellow-orange colour when you apply the seal. Alternatively, you can stain the boards in one of the many brilliant colours now available. The great advantage of stains is that they add welcome colour to a dull room and don't conceal the grain of the wood.

As with every other decorating job, preparation is all important. Examine the floor for nails sticking out of the boards. Knock them in with a hammer and take out any bent ones with a clawhammer or pliers. For your neighbours' sake, keep your hammering to the daytime. Small gaps in the boards can be filled with *papier mâché* which can be made quite simply. Tear a newspaper into small pieces and then soak the pieces in water. Squeeze them out and add this soggy mess to some glue size, mixed rather stronger than it says on the packet. Don't let the mixture become too set. Press it with a knife into the gaps between the floorboards, forcing it well down. This is quick and cheap and has the same entertainment value as mud pies.

If the gaps are too wide for this treatment, swallowing up the mixture completely, cut slivers of wood (not more than 3 feet (90 cm) long) and glue them into the gaps. If the floor is warped or in very bad condition, sanding is a simple, quick and cheap way of straightening it out. This is useful even if you don't intend to seal, because other floor coverings like cork, vinyl, carpet or even rugs, should have a smooth surface beneath them.

A floor sander looks something like a big vacuum cleaner. They are not a great pleasure to use because of the noise, the vibration and the dust they make, but sanding itself is not hard and is a satisfactory and cheap way to produce good-looking, versatile flooring which will last a long time. The machine can be hired from a local tool hire shop. Use a coarse abrasive sheet to begin with, gradually using finer ones until the floor is smooth.

Condensation

Have you ever been in a bathroom where large blobs of water collect on the ceiling and drop coldly on to your exposed parts when having a bath? That's condensation and it can happen anywhere in the house. It is commonest in the bathroom or kitchen where steam turns to vapour and collects on cold surfaces, such as windows, walls and ceilings where there's no central heating. Eventually it rots window frames and makes the wallpaper mouldy, but it is unpleasant to live with anyway.

The cure is to see that the room is warm and has some air flowing through. An extractor fan will help, and so will air vents and louvre-topped windows. Improving the insulation will also help, as will having warm surfaces and some form of efficient heating. Cork is a 'warm' material often used as insulation, so it can help greatly where there is condensation. Ceilings covered in flame retardant expanded polystyrene tiles will help to insulate the room; so will walls covered with sheet expanded polystyrene, sold in rolls. You can wallpaper over this or if you don't want pattern, use lining paper and paint over that. You can paint emulsion directly on to polystyrene, but it's very soft and vulnerable on its own. Never use gloss paint on it. Nothing will truly cure condensation unless you have adequate ventilation and warmth.

This may look amusing but it spells disaster, discomfort and rot. Condensation will only disappear if you can provide warmth and ventilation.

Stairs

Stairs become worn if there's no carpet on them and then they can be dangerous, specially to the very young, the very old and people in high heels. It's possible to cut out the worn section and splice in a new section which is far, far cheaper than replacing the treads. Squeeze glue into the crack and clamp the parts together in position. If the crack is large you may have to wedge a bit of dowel into it as well. The more you can make do with wedges and glue the better because new balusters cost a fortune. Sand the new pieces down when you've finished. Most staircases and balusters are painted and often there's a really nice plain wood underneath. It is the patient work of some weeks to get rid of all this paint, but it's a soothing job that can be done gradually. If you don't like this back-to-the-earth basic look paint the stairs in a fashionable sugared almond colour — or timeless white.

Draughtproofing

This is one of the easiest, cheapest and most rewarding forms of ensuring home comfort. You know by now, of course, that the typical home loses 75 per cent of its heating through the roof, walls and floors, so three-quarters of the money you spend on heating is going to warm up the sparrows on the roof. Of course there are sophisticated and expensive ways of seeing this doesn't happen, but there

The pleasing appearance of a sanded floor takes time and effort to achieve, but as you can see, it's well worth it.

Small sanding machines like this can be hired quite cheaply. They can be used for sanding furniture as well as the edges and corners of a floor.

are also several highly effective and extremely cheap things you can do which will make a difference, not just to the heating bill but also to your comfort.

In the first place you can block up all the draughts from doors and windows. If you want to find out where these are, hold your hand over the window frames and the door frames one chilly autumn day and see where a blast of cold air hits it. Sticky tape is an effective way to stop the draught. Masking tape is fairly inoffensive to look at and will probably peel off again in the spring without dragging all the paint with it. Otherwise of course you can buy rolls of self-stick foam insulation which are specially designed for windows. This should mean you can go on opening the window during winter, though I personally prefer to be hermetically sealed during the cold months (allowing some air to get in for breathing, of course).

There are various insulation strips available for doors and, again if you hold your hand up you will feel exactly where the cold air is getting in. Other places where draughts can affect the warmth and comfort are down chimneys, through bath plugs and waste outlets, through letter boxes and floorboards (but of course, you will be filling those with *papier mâché* as described on page 25 won't you?). Overflow pipes can be temporarily blocked with the neck of a toy balloon (a sort of birth-control for draughts). If you have a roof, insulate it. You may be able to get a grant for this. There are various forms of roof insulation available. I am still using the piece of flooring felt I picked up off the street where an office was being refurbished, and that was twenty years ago. The cold water tank which used to freeze up every winter has never done so since.

4 · Specific arrangements

In ideal circumstances a home is carefully planned round the lives and tastes of the people living in it with a balance of design, colour, texture and general style. For many people the reality of planning a home means fitting in with what's there already and trying to make do with borrowed, inherited or second-hand furniture or whatever the landlord has seen fit to put into the place. It also means making do with impractical plumbing, badly arranged fitments and hideous carpet.

You can beat all this by being a bit ingenious and treating the whole thing as a challenge. Let's take some of the more common problems and look at them separately.

Entrance

You come home and open the front door – what do you see? A dimly lit, cold, grubby and dismal space with murky stairs and a flutter of promotional cards from the local plumber or taxi firm lying on the mat.

It's not always easy to see what you can do about the particular seediness of a hall of this kind, especially if you are sharing it with people in other flats in the house. But a coat of say, sunflower yellow paint, would help for a start if you can get agreement from all the people concerned and contributions from your upstairs and downstairs neighbours. Get hold of a cheap Numdah or Kelim rug in cheerful colours and the place will look more welcoming at once.

Most important of all is probably the lighting. A brighter bulb in the fitting will make a big difference and so will a respectable lampshade. The ubiquitous Chinese paper globes are always good to look at, give a pleasant light and are excellent value. Recently some square, Japanese-type paper shades have come on to the market and they make a stylish alternative.

Find a few old pictures in a charity shop or jumble sale, take them out of their frames and throw them away. Put your own prints or paintings in the frames instead and hang them in a group on the wall. Add, if you can, a shelf for post, messages and gloves, wider or narrower as the space permits, and as large a mirror as you can afford. Mirrors reflect whatever light there is and give the appear-

This long, narrow hall was pretty dark until the owners installed a glazed door at the far end. The church pew provides seating and boot-changing space without taking up too much room.

The dismal and poorly organized kitchen (below right) was transformed into the bright and welcoming space (below) by using a bold colour scheme and adding matching accessories.

Right: This is a very dark kitchen overshadowed by a large tree. The mirror was bought very cheaply at a local auction and practically doubles the light as well as the size of the room.

Brightness and an illusion of space has been added to a dismal lavatory by painting a trompe-l'oeil *window on one wall. The curved edge* (far left) *is caused by the special lens used to take the photograph.*

ance of space. Mirror tiles can be bought cheaply from decorating shops and you can tack a wooden frame, or paint a frame round them later. Put some dried flowers in a jug on the shelf and coming home will be a better experience. If you scour junk shops and jumble sales you should be able to get an old-fashioned hat stand with a trough for umbrellas as well as pegs for hats and coats. If space is really limited, the best answer could be to hang up a bamboo framed mirror with lots of knobs sticking out for hats and scarves.

Long, narrow passages are less easy to deal with. Mirrors are the best solution for giving an impression of width and it helps to paint the walls in a pale colour. The ubiquitous magnolia has a pinkish tinge; if you want to avoid that, you could use a muffin colour, but there are plenty of pastels around. If you change to a darker colour two-thirds of the way up the walls you will diminish the sense of height and narrowness in the passage. Try painting a *trompe-l'oeil* picture to give an impression of perspective and distance, such as an avenue of trees or a window with a view, and reflect it in a mirror opposite.

Kitchen

Other people's dirt is always much worse than one's own, and other people's kitchens are always left in a dreadful state. So I'm afraid the first thing you will have to do is get down on your hands and knees and clean and scrub using all the cleaning devices known to hardware shops until you can really see the problems through the grime. Then you can assess what you must do to make the kitchen habitable.

Kitchens in purpose-designed flats are often quite practical, though usually small and rather characterless. Kitchens in converted houses, however, are usually very small, often awkward in shape and not always very conveniently placed because they have been put where they are simply to be near whatever plumbing already exists in the house. Often they have too many doors, or doors and windows in the wrong places, or they may have an odd alcove for no reason except that it used to be a fireplace or a niche for the boiler. These things make it very difficult to plan the kitchen to be convenient. The best course, if possible, is to behave as though these impediments don't exist. If the door is not necessary, close it off for good and treat it as part of the wall. Equally, if you've racked your brains as to what to do with an intriguing looking alcove and nothing seems quite right, ignore it. Put in a table or a trolley or a kitchen unit, in line with the other cupboards and not pushed back into the space. This will make for a much more practical kitchen and perhaps you can find a tiny set of shelves or put a print or a poster in the alcove for pure decoration.

Cheap kitchen units (and you are not likely to find expensive ones in a dump) often have no backs, thus leaving a way open for mice and draughts. If you can, get a piece of hardboard cut to fit and fix it to the back to block off what you can of the pipes and other excrescences inside. Then cover the cupboard floor with a washable

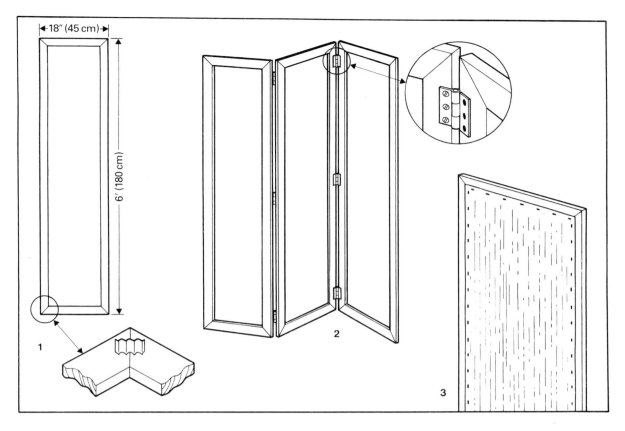

surface, perhaps vinyl to match the rest of the kitchen floor. The cupboard will be much easier to clean and the kitchen will have a more unified look.

When your kitchen is clean and orderly buy a coloured plastic bowl for the sink; this saves on hot water and won't clatter when you wash up. Match it with a cutlery drainer, soap dish and bucket and the kitchen will begin to be more like your own and less like the landlord's.

Problem kitchens come in all shapes and sizes.

Small, mean and narrow

This is the sort of kitchen where if you bend down to take the chicken out of the oven your bottom hits the cupboards on the opposite wall. If you can manage to do with cupboards on only one wall and just a worktop on the other the whole thing will feel more spacious. Always try to have as much worktop space as possible, specially since there almost certainly won't be room for a table. A narrow shelf above the worktop will hold small spice and herb jars, salt and pepper, small tins, small vases: the things you use often and want to be able to get at quickly. On wider shelves they would get hidden behind larger objects.

Very tall

Very tall kitchens are often found in converted houses where the high ceiling used to be in proportion with the larger room. Such a

To make a screen

1   Using 2 × 1 inch (5 × 2 cm) wood, cut two 6 ft (180 cm) lengths and two 18 inch (45 cm) lengths for each frame of the screen. Cut 45° angles at each corner and fasten the frame together with corrugated screws.
2   Screw hinges to the frames as shown above, making sure that the screen is able to bend in a Z shape.
3   Staple or tack canvas, gingham, denim or any firm fabric to each side of the frame, about 1 inch (2 cm) from the edges. Before tacking, remember to turn under the raw edges of the fabric to prevent them fraying.

Right: *This attic bathroom makes full use of light and colour and its peculiar shape to give a smart Victorian-style bathroom.*

Left: *A very small lavatory in a high-rise flat is made cheerful by a bold use of yellow. Even the bottle of disinfectant matches!*

Far left: *This silly goose drinking the water out of the cistern was painted by a friend in his tiny lavatory. The cheerful yellow beak is matched by the yellow boats.*

Left and above left: *Life in a small room can be made more bearable by installing a simple, but efficient room divider. Keeping it below ceiling height leaves the appearance of space.*

Above: *The worktop acts as an effective room divider and doubles up as a breakfast bar.*

Left: *A cramped cooking area in a multi-purpose room can be a nightmare if it is disorganized. Try to keep it neat and clean or you'll be living in permanent chaos like this.*

Left: *An ancient and uninviting bathroom sometimes needs more than a coat of paint! The simple blue scheme (above) with coordinating tiles and careful choice of accessories turns it into a very civilized bathroom.*

ceiling is a good excuse for installing an old-fashioned clothes airer on a pulley. An enterprising firm has begun to make these again (see address section) but you can sometimes find the metal bits and pulley contraption at jumble sales or in junk shops. All you need add are four thin poles from a timber shop to be able to haul your smalls up and down at will; then the bath need not always be overhung with dripping washing.

To lessen the effect of the high ceiling you can run a shelf round fairly high up, and keep decorative plates on it. To lessen the actual height, you can tack wooden slats across to battens fixed to the wall, effectively bringing the ceiling lower. Then you can recess 'downlights' behind the slats for gentle background light and put in spotlights or wall lights for working by.

Kitchen-in-a-corner

Very often, one's thoughtful landlord has provided a sort of 'cooking centre' at one end of the living-room. Sometimes this is on the open-plan basis with maybe a waist-high room divider which acts as the bedhead-bedtable on one side and the kitchen cupboard on the other. The height of this divider may vary or there may be no divider at all, but basically what it means is that one end of the room is the kitchen and the other the bedroom, and if the room is big enough there may be somewhere to sit as well.

Your first resolution must be to keep all equipment to an absolute minimum and the second is to have only good-looking equipment which you can count as decoration. Get the prettiest plates and the most decorative utensils. One way of separating the kitchen is to find or make a tall screen and use this as the dividing line. Second-hand screens are hard to find and new ones expensive. Make your own by tacking four pieces of wood into a frame, stretching and stapling fabric over it. Make two or three of these and hinge them together. You can then paint or varnish the screen, cover it with fabric or collage, or stencil on to it.

It's perfectly possible to curtain off the kitchen, certainly in a large room, but there's a sort of unwholesome feeling about curtained-off areas; they seem grubby and the fabric inevitably becomes greasy and drab. So be positive; accept and incorporate the kitchen into your room and make something of it. Put food into glass containers, display tins in neat rows, get brightly coloured bowls, pans and china, and keep everything clean and neat. Be disciplined. Throw out rubbish regularly and don't collect unnecessary objects. Tiny refrigerators are available, mainly designed for caravans but just as good for bedsits, and quite large enough to keep the milk and fish fingers from going off.

Light the separate areas of your room with separate lamps so that you can leave an area in the dark or only dimly lit and enjoy the feeling of being apart from the 'kitchen' or 'work area' when you want to entertain or eat chocolates or do your fingernails. If you have the choice, choose to have the kitchen area close to a window to let out cooking smells.

Small though this area may be, you will have to find places to store most of your cleaning equipment in it so you must be ingenious. A small shelf or wall cupboard will hold household cleaners and cloths. Long handled equipment such as brooms can be hung on the wall between two pegs.

An ironing board can also be hung on the wall, or you can have a let-down ironing board hinged against the wall or opening out of a cupboard. The iron can be mounted on a specially designed stand available from department stores that saves space and also makes it safer to put the iron away while it is still hot.

Keep only one of everything you need and throw away clogged up jars of household cleaners. Keep them beneath the sink in a plastic bowl (or if there are small children, on a high shelf) which you can then sort out from time to time.

Bathroom

Bathrooms and lavatories are usually miniscule, often windowless and sometimes difficult to keep warm. They are the rooms least likely to have been given any serious consideration at the planning stage of a conversion and even in new houses the bathroom is not given much space or real thought. Some grand houses have enormous bathrooms with huge freestanding baths set down confidently on four legs right in the middle of the highly-polished floor. In the affluent households they were created for, bathrooms like this were heated by a log fire and there was plenty of room to lounge in an armchair and store all the paraphernalia for dressing.

You may not be aiming that high with your small bathroom, but you can keep in mind the sort of thinking that says a bathroom should have style and comfort. Your bathroom should be interesting, warm and practical. Even hopelessly old-fashioned bathrooms offer possibilities. They are full of pipes which you can paint in contrasting colours to the rest of the room, incorporating them into the decoration instead of trying to pretend they are not there. A friend of mine in a London flat painted the pipe leading into the lavatory cistern to look like a goose's neck. Another friend in a thirteen-storey block of flats has painted her bathroom the brightest blue with bright red pipes.

An ugly bath can be covered with cork tiles to match the floor, or boxed in with hardboard covered in anything you like: paint, tiles (ceramic, vinyl or cork), fabric or paper. No matter how small the bathroom, fit a mirror somewhere and make sure it's well lit. Then you can do all your make up and/or shaving there and won't need to clutter up the rest of your home with bottles and brushes. A big mirror or mirror tiles over the bath will immediately double the apparent size of the room which makes for a less claustrophobic atmosphere.

Don't be afraid to hang pictures on the walls — unless, of course, they're priceless oil paintings which might warp. One city dweller I know has filled her bathroom with rather romantic framed pictures of peasant women in the fields — originally Victorian advertisements for fruit and vegetables.

A very small lavatory can be decorated with a collage using

Right: *This platform bed with storage underneath is not very appealing or successful. Organizing a small space in this way calls for neatness and discipline as seen in both platforms opposite.*

Above: *The height of this attic room has been used to install a platform for a double bed. The cover is a patchwork quilt made by friends as a wedding present.*

Right: *A supremely elegant chrome platform creates a bedspace, leaving room below for a comfortable sitting-room. The simplicity is emphasized by having only a mattress and some plants on the platform.*

Left: *This room is unashamedly pretty in a particularly English way. The prints, though different, complement each other, the fabrics are crisp and clean-looking and the white painted furniture is reminiscent of nurseries or country cottages. The flowers, of course, should always be fresh.*

pictures out of the colour supplements. Mostly these marvellous photographs get thrown away and forgotten very quickly. They can be preserved for a short posterity if you paste them up on the wall. You can have a completely random set of cut out pictures, juxtapose them to look humorous or concentrate on a theme: cars, trains, fruit and vegetables or nudes. Alternatively you can get in there with a paintbrush and do your own thing. If you hate it you can always try again.

If the flat has no bathroom, you might be able to fit a shower in somewhere. I know of two London homes which have tiny square hip baths in a space under the stairs.

There is a convention which says that baths and basins have to be in pastel colours so you will probably be stuck with palest yellow, dirty white or eau de nil. If you don't like the colour of the fittings ignore them and concentrate your energies on the walls. If you can afford to change them, there are plenty of dark and interesting colours available. If you like pastels, you have nothing to worry about, you can paint the walls pale pink the ceiling ice-cream blue and the floor primrose.

Multi-purpose rooms

This is often a polite name for the good old bedsit. It's truly amazing what many landlords imagine you can squeeze into one tiny room: bed, wardrobe, dining and work table, kitchen, hand basin (which, of course, doubles as a sink), leaving very little room for the person. Rooms which have to act as everything deserve careful thought. They seem to work best if they are kept entirely simple with no unnecessary junk – unless you have the lucky knack of being able to collect bits and pieces and put them together so that your room is like an old patchwork or a collage.

If you are in furnished accommodation, the chances are your taste and the landlord's will not coincide in any respect. He will have put in any old furniture he can lay his hands on cheaply, from splay-legged tables which trip you up to enormous wardrobes which gobble up space without being beautiful and whose doors won't open fully in the space allotted to them. If you can get rid of some of it, do so. It's far better to have too little furniture than to have too much. Perhaps there's a space under the stairs or in the corridor where it can be stored until the landlord removes it or you leave and can put it back.

If you're stuck with everything, don't despair. There are several things you can do to comouflage furniture. Ugly tables can be covered by cloths. A cheap covering can be made of remnants or old curtains or bits of lace, but there's no rule about the sort of fabric you can use. Something washable is best, but anything from sewn-together teacloths, through furnishing velvet to dress fabrics can look good. An old-fashioned idea that has come back into favour is to put two cloths one on top of the other – a plain one underneath and a smaller, patterned one on top. This not only looks charming, it also disguises a multitude of landlord sins.

Dark colours and patterns tend to be more practical because they hide tomato ketchup and spilled coffee stains and save on trips to the launderette. In fact you can use fabric to cover all sorts of blots on the landscape. Your bed could be clothed during the day in a crocheted blanket, a horse blanket, a tablecloth, a patchwork quilt or a duvet with a non-bedroomy design. Windows can be curtained with gingham or old lace tablecloths, muslin, Laura Ashley or cheap market fabrics, or actual curtains from a jumble sale.

A small room will present plenty of practical problems, but there's no need for it to look cramped. Deep colours tend to give the impression of coming forward to meet you and pale ones the effect of receding. So if you paint a room in pale colours it will seem larger; if you paint a ceiling a paler colour than the walls it will seem to be higher and give the room an added feeling of spaciousness.

Shiny surfaces also help to give a feeling of space, and though you won't want your living-room to have the high gloss of a public lavatory, there are plenty of semi-gloss and eggshell paints which give a pleasant finish.

Wallpapers with a strong directional pattern can help to 'push out' walls. Horizontal stripes will make a room seem wide; vertical stripes will produce an impression of height. If you are using patterned wall coverings or carpet, choose a pale background if you want to add to the general feeling of space.

A friend of mine papered his flat in wide green and white stripes, looking through an arch to narrow stripes of the same colour, and this difference in width gave a completely contrived but successful impression of space to his tiny flat.

Many divided rooms have ceilings that are too high in proportion to their diminished size. A strong, dark colour in the ceiling will help to bring it 'nearer'. Soft, matt surfaces and bold, solid colours will diminish the sense of space. Matching patterned wallpapers, curtains and covers (whether bed or chair) will give an immediately 'cosy' effect and help to give a coordinated feeling to a room full of bits and pieces.

If space is scarce, which of course it will be, no matter how large the room, try to find furniture which is light or on wheels so that you can move it round easily. For instance, you could hang your clothes on a clothes rail on wheels, available from clothing shop suppliers. Many a clothes rail has been filched out of a street skip to serve a useful purpose as somebody's wardrobe.

Folding chairs are many and varied, and some are as comfortable as traditional chairs. You can hang them on the wall when you are not using them, where they look decorative and are out of the way. A big basket or a painted dustbin can be used for dirty clothes waiting for the launderette.

If the room is tall you may be able to fix a platform which will add what amounts to virtually another room, and will also give a rather dull room some interest. Even in rooms of smaller proportions platforms can be useful.

You can ring the changes with platforms in many ways. The space underneath can be used as a sitting area, a hanging area for clothes, a storage area with a completely enclosed cupboard or a study area

The light and well-proportioned room on the left was an uninviting space until a coordinated colour scheme of pink and frills (above) *made it into a very feminine bedroom.*

Right: *Full length curtains must be lined and have plenty of fullness if they are to hang well. These are finished with a deep pelmet.*

with a desk. If you work at home, you can squeeze a very satisfactory little work space against one wall or part of a wall of your room. A door or a wide shelf resting on two filing cabinets or chests of drawers can be used as a work surface or as an integral part of a shelving system. Pinboard and shelving fixed above and beside this work area will ensure everything you need is at hand. An adjustable typist's chair is excellent for people who sit at their work for long periods, but many of the cheap, folding chairs available are quite comfortable for a little while. A good working light is essential. The best is probably an angled lamp which you can get from office suppliers and department stores. However, any lamp which lights up your work without casting shadows or glaring in your face will be perfectly adequate.

Living-rooms

Single-purpose rooms are easier to decorate than multi-purpose because there's less going on in them, less clutter, less furniture and they have a more specific function. This allows you to play with pattern in a less inhibited way. However, beware of large patterns. These require large expanses of wall or floor to achieve the full effect, they must match up perfectly at the joins and they need a fairly stylish or stately setting.

Small patterns can be used much more easily and with good effect. If you have large windows and hanker after boldness, use it on the curtains, but match them up with a smaller version on the walls or with carefully coordinating colours.

Curtains in general help to give a room a 'dressy' look, so don't be mean with them. They should reach to the ground unless covering a tiny window or a radiator, and should pull right back to the edge of the wall. If you can't afford curtains, use roller blinds as they accentuate the shape of well-proportioned windows, can be made of any fabric (see page 96) or designed to order. Curtains that tone or match with pale walls will give a lighter look to the room, whereas contrasting curtains frame the window more dramatically.

Bedrooms

For some reason there's a convention that bedrooms should be 'pretty' in a rather little-girl way with dimity prints and frills. This is one of the easiest effects to achieve. Pick your preferred pale colour and print, and cover walls, floor, windows and bed with it. It's hard to go wrong.

If you prefer something a little more restrained and classic, pick your colour and add a contrasting colour judiciously. The contrast could simply be a different tone of the same colour or something startlingly different. It depends whether you want to vamp it up or use the room for peace and quiet.

If you want exoticism or eroticism, go for deep red or black velvet or satin and moody lights with coloured shades or bulbs. The great advantage of a separate bedroom, as far as decorating is concerned, is that it all centres round the bed, so you can concentrate on a particular whim, feeling or mood, using the bed dramatically, like a stage set.

Child's room or play area

Living in a small space with a young child is not easy. You are under each other's feet all day, it's almost impossible to keep everything tidy and your interests clash.

If you have to begin by sharing the bedroom with your child, think of the advantages; for example, you can lean across and comfort the baby in the middle of the night without having to get out of bed. Most nursing mothers find it very convenient to have the crib next to their own bed and, of course, it's cheaper in winter than having to heat a separate room for the baby. If you want a little privacy, put up a screen (see page 33). A very young baby doesn't need much space. A small cot, a storage unit and something comfortable to sit on for feeding are the only pieces of furniture necessary. There should also be space on the floor or somewhere for the baby to lie and kick and grab and talk to you and look around.

As the baby gets older, the space problems multiply. It is quite astonishing how much a small baby can acquire in the way of possessions. Many people nowadays use disposable nappies, but even so, clothes alone can take up drawerfuls of space. A chest of drawers exclusively for the baby will soon be a necessity. You'll also notice that toys come crowding in from all quarters and you have to find homes for them. They can be kept in boxes with hinged lids (see page 80) which can also be used as seating and soft toys can be bundled into a big basket or arranged in a group as though they were a football team about to have their photographs taken. It is best to find separate storage for different types of toy so that the large things don't crush the smaller ones and you can actually find a set of paints and pens all together and ready to use, not jumbled up among a million other items.

As the child gets older and wants places to play in, look at the space under the stairs and see if it can't be made into a cosy little play house. It will need to be well lit and warm and fitted with things the child will appreciate, not just any old junk. Children are very quick to know when they're being fobbed off with rubbish and when a thing is really worthwhile. A toy telephone, a little desk and chair, a toy stove with pans, paintings (their own and others people's), and posters, can be pinned to the walls. You might be tempted to go and play in it yourself.

Another possible play area is a landing. Here you will have to see to draughtproofing and heating in order to make it warm and cosy. When very young children are around it is a good idea to put up a gate, though that needn't cost a lot. My daughter used one side of a drop-sided cot for her little girl, wedging it between the bannister and the wall. It was absolutely safe and cost nothing at all.

A child's room should be simple, fun and have plenty of open storage and lots of room to play in. This blue room fulfills all the conditions.

Safety for children

Children are greatly at risk in their own homes. Being unsteady on their feet and inexperienced in the dangers of life, they can slip, trip, poison, cut, burn or electrocute themselves very easily. Obviously you cannot eliminate all dangers but you can foresee many of them and prevent them from happening. For instance, you can tape up the socket outlets you are not using at any one time to stop a baby poking his fingers or a knitting needle down the holes. You can make sure there are no trailing electric leads lying across the floor and that you never, never leave the iron on and plugged in while you go to answer the door. You can make sure the house is well lit, especially on the stairs and you can keep all household products, many of which are poisonous, on a high shelf away from the child. You can put a lockable cupboard in the kitchen or bathroom to store all aspirin and other medicines and you can turn the saucepan handles towards the cooker and never let the child into the cooking area. One house we rented had the large kitchen divided at waist height so my son could play within sight of me but never be in danger from the activities and objects in the working area. The room divider was also useful on the kitchen side to store glasses, plates and cutlery.

5 · Difficult shapes and awkward corners

Nearly all houses have awkward shapes somewhere, spaces under the stairs or under sloping roofs, spaces where the light can never get in or odd little alcoves which are too small to act as rooms but too obvious to pretend they are not there. The square boxes which modern building allows the dweller are, oddly enough, awkward because of their simplicity, allowing no space for storage or personal idiosyncracies. Here we shall creep under stairs and stoop under roofs and suggest ways of using them to their best advantage, or at least making the best of a bad job.

Attics and sloping roofs

Attics are usually chilly in winter because the roof space is often not insulated. If you are lucky, warmth will rise from the flats below and heat the space a little. On the other hand, attics are liable to be like ovens in the summer when the sun beats down on the roof and there's nowhere for the heat to escape. So one thing to do is insulate if you can. A decorative and fairly effective way of insulating is to fix cork tiles to the sloping walls and ceiling. You can get thick, rather loose dark brown cork insulating tiles from DIY shops and these are easily stuck on the wall. They exude a strong smell of cork at first, but they can be sealed. Alternatively they can be painted white if you find the dark colour a little too gloomy. Such tiles are useful not just for insulation but also for pinning up postcards, pictures, reminders, birthday cards and can solve the jewellery storage problem very well.

If you think this sounds a bit dull and you want something more feminine, you can wallpaper the whole room in a tiny, sprigged print – better in such a confined space than something large and overbearing – and take up one of the colours in the paper when you paint the window frames, skirtings and doors. The thing is to have as little clutter as possible for your basic scheme when space is so limited, so you don't end up with a mass of confusion and no idea where anything is. If you are using the room as a bedsitter you can take advantage of the low ceiling to pin up fabric and give yourself a canopy for the bed.

Attics usually have quite small windows, often of the 'mansard' type which jut out of the roof, making a little alcove in the room which may be delightful to look at, but difficult to find a use for. If the radiator has been installed under the window of this alcove it will not be doing its job very well because the heat will escape out of the window before it has time to filter into the room. Putting a strip of silver foil behind the radiator can help to reflect the heat into the room but it won't make a lot of difference. If you have any say where the radiator is to go, suggest a different wall than the one with the window in it. A good use for an indented window space is to put a table there at working height where you can eat, sew, type or study. You will get the benefit of the light plus the warmth from the radiator if it's there.

Very often the attic window will be sloping so that curtains look silly. In this case use a roller blind with a hook at the bottom. This prevents it dangling down and keeps draughts out more efficiently.

If the roof comes down very low to the floor, make sure that the low end is used for activities where you won't bump your head. Put cushions or low chairs against that wall, or place a desk there and sit facing the wall so your head won't come into contact with the slope. Put your bed at the low end, too; the lower the bed the better. A mattress on the floor might be the best idea, or you might prefer to buy a Japanese futon which can be folded up as a sofa during the day. A low bed on castors can be wheeled under the eaves during the day and pulled out at night, though this is not a very satisfactory arrangement if you want to use the bed every night, unless you are an extraordinarily neat person.

Attics lend themselves to flexible and informal living. Floor cushions can be lined against the wall and used for lounging to watch television and for seating guests. The television itself (if you have one) should be put on a low table so that people sitting on the floor can watch in comfort.

No space for a wardrobe? Try an old-fashioned bentwood hatstand. You can get these second-hand in old office equipment shops, but now they are made new and sold in smart, young furniture stores. You will have to size the room up to see where there will be enough height to take it – not in front of the window or the door, for instance, though it might not matter if it had to stand in front of some shelves.

Since storage is going to be a problem look around the room and see where you could fit a row of boxes which can be used for seating as well as storage (see page 80). Covered in a fabric to match the blinds and bedcover they could be English Country Pretty; left their natural colour and sealed they could be Scandinavian Classic; painted in primary colours they could be High Tech. Whatever you do, they'll come in useful for hiding bedlinen and pillows. Boxes like this can sit under the low ceiling without disturbing the rest of the arrangements and double as seating if you keep them low.

Other useful things are hooks. You can get cheap little plastic hooks to self-stick on to a wall, though they are not very decorative and won't take much weight. Better than these are the expanding trellis arrangements with wooden knobs, which look decorative in their own right and are invaluable for storing things like hats, scarves, beads and so on.

All this refers to attics which have been converted. You may have your eye on an unconverted roof space, but you will probably find there's no adequate ventilation or light and that the floor consists of hardboard or even cardboard laid over the joists which will burst through into the room below if you place a foot on it. Altogether, such spaces must be professionally converted to be useable.

Basements

My first flat ever was in a basement in Edinburgh. You had to go down the area steps, along a little concrete way, into a side door, through a dark little passage with the loo on one side and a minute cupboard with a bath in it on the other. Eventually you reached the small living-room with a tiny little kitchen and a bedroom off it. It was dirty, decrepit and dark, but you could climb out of the window in the morning to eat breakfast in the garden where there was an apple tree, lots of grass, a washing line and a place to put the paddling pool. In December it received only a glimmer of winter sunlight, but in summer we could spend all day out in the open.

Such are the advantages and disadvantages of most basements. Without some sort of garden they are dank and miserable indeed, but the garden can transform the dingiest of cellars into a home.

The worst difficulties are usually damp, cold and darkness. When you've located the damp and done something to cure it, i.e. mended the gutter or the roof, or blocked off the rising damp or had the bricks repointed (see chapter 3) you can cover up the damage. If you are in a position to replaster, so much the better. If not, you will have to see what camouflage can do. You may need several coats of paint to cover up brown patches on wall or ceiling where the damp has been getting through, specially if you choose a pale colour. It would probably be better to paper the walls first. A favourite paper at the moment is wood chip which has an irregular textured surface that conceals absolutely every imperfection. To some eyes, however, it is am imperfection in itself. But covered with a colour of your choice, it looks quite acceptable, and since you will need to put things on the walls in order to store them, you probably won't see much of it anyway.

Another device for concealing damp and ugly patches is to grow a jungle of plants. You can hang plants from the ceiling to conceal the place where the upstairs washing-machine overflowed; you can grow a tall plant in front of a patch of plaster made bubbly from ancient damp coming in from outside; you can use posters, wall hangings or an old dresser to cover up large areas of ugliness. The advantage of these measures is that when you leave you can simply unpin them or pick them up and take them away with you, whereas the paint and the paper, of course, have to be left behind.

Use fan heaters and some ventilation, through the window if necessary, to move the air about and get rid of any damp. This will help you get rid of condensation which can be a problem in basements. If the floor feels particularly cold or damp, use nice warm rugs for your poor feet. Numdah rugs, embroidered in India, are

beautifully soft and warm to walk on, very pretty to look at and remarkably cheap from charity shops and other outlets. Rush matting may also make the place more comfortable and warm-feeling though this is less easy to clean.

Getting enough light into the place may well be a problem. The sort of basement dinge, caused through overshadowing by pavements and buildings, can be very depressing. However, it's not an insurmountable problem. Use mirrors wherever you can, placed so that they reflect what light there is and where you can see them. They can almost double the amount of light if you take care where you put them and if there's any view to reflect, they can bring that

The chaotic study above becomes an efficient workroom (far left, above) *when well-organized storage is arranged in the narrow space.*

A dark and decrepit basement can be transformed into a sunny and welcoming room by using shades of yellow and a pale floor to maximize the light.

Far left, below: *Cube storage makes the best of a very small space; it acts as bed, drawer and cupboard storage, and as a bedside table.*

inside as well. Use colour to counteract the basement gloom too. Yellow is not easy to use as it doesn't always cover well. However, corn yellow is a warm colour that can give an impression of sun like no other colour on earth.

In order to let in as much natural light as possible, don't block a single ray of light coming through the window by using curtains. It's much better to use blinds. If you really feel overlooked by the world, use very sheer fabric for the curtains or blinds and make sure you can pull them right back from the window.

If the window lets in little light and looks out on to a horrible view of dustbins and litter, conceal the whole thing behind shelves. On these you can put plants, which will be glad of the light, or glasses and coloured glass objects that will catch the smallest ray and shine like jewels. Wooden or chipboard shelves are suitable for plants, but glass shelves look spectacular for glass objects.

In basement kitchens the stale air is liable to hang around and remind you unpleasantly of the fried eggs, bacon and chips you had earlier in the evening. An extractor fan is a worthwhile expense to prevent this, and also helps to get rid of the dreaded condensation. Modern fans are made in a range of fruit gum colours which make them, if not things of beauty, at least acceptable carbuncles on the face of the window. Silica gel, available from chemists, can be put into the cupboards to absorb any damp which persists there.

Under the stairs

This is a much neglected area. Very often it's full only of carrier bags, half pairs of gloves, perished winter boots, ancient holdalls and crumpled anoraks. Worse, it will almost certainly be unlit so there's little incentive to rummage about and discover its potential.

However, it can be a useful little storage area. My sister boxed hers in leaving a door and used it to store all her tinned foodstuffs. In her tiny kitchen it solved a serious space problem and made use of an otherwise useless space. The best light to install is an angled or spot lamp fixed to the wall or clamped to a shelf. An automatic device can be bought from most electrical shops which switches the light on when you open the door and turns it off when you close it.

Depending on the steepness of the stairs and how much space there is under them, you might be able to fix a phone to the wall and put the directories with a pencil and notebook on a small shelf unit or table below. A low chair will make telephoning more comfortable and a good light will help to make the space properly useable. In this case, of course, you won't have to box the thing in. If you don't want to encourage long phone calls, don't heat the space. Otherwise you could fix a wall heater on a time switch, or a wall heater and light combined as used in bathrooms.

Another use for this space is as storage for cleaning equipment; hooks and clips on the wall make it possible to hang most things off the ground which makes them easy to get at and easier to put away. They won't then be in a clutter on the floor and you can clean under them.

If you fix a neat set of shelves under the stairs you can use them to keep your books, household files, shoe cleaning materials and gardening tools, scraps for patchwork – it all depends on your interests, but I defy anybody with any interests not to find some use for this seldom-used space, provided it has been carefully planned and designed.

If you're really stumped for ideas, remember that under the stairs is a good place to put hyacinth bulbs while waiting for them to produce those three inches of green leaf which they need before you bring them out into the light for Christmas.

Making a window seat
Much of this scheme can be made using an upright and bracket shelving system. The bookcase sides can be nailed on to the shelves, provided you won't want to adjust them later. The seat itself can be made from foam and covered with hard-wearing fabric fixed in place with a staple gun.

Landings

Many landings, especially in old Victorian houses are quite spacious and very wasted. Theoretically they'd make good places for 'doing' something in. Unfortunately, they are also usually open to the stairwell which is draughty, cold and public so that to work or do anything quiet there would be intolerably difficult and unpleasant. However, if your lifestyle has to be cramped into one room and you are seriously short of space, it might be possible to find uses for this area which would release some space in your own room.

Shoe-cleaning can be done there, or you could store your sewing things or other items of equipment. A bookcase could hold paperbacks if your bookshelves are bulging already. At any rate, you can

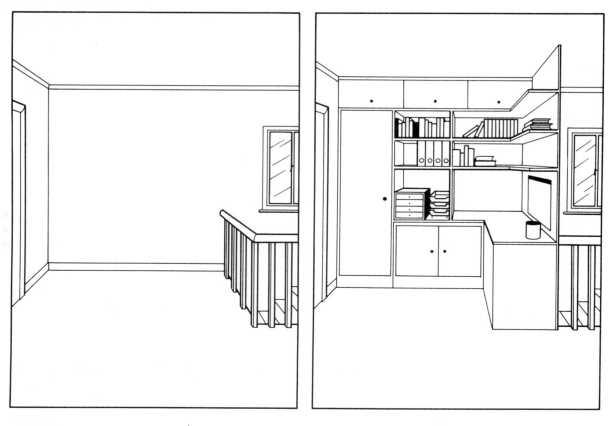

Converting a landing

A landing can be made to 'pay its way' by installing shelving and cupboards to take some of the overspill from elsewhere in your home. If heated, it can be a cosy work or hobby area.

Above & top, opposite: The transformation from gloomy basement to farmhouse kitchen was inexpensively achieved with second-hand furniture, cheap pine units and a vinyl floor.

make it a good deal pleasanter to negotiate on your way home than it probably was when you found it. In the first place, a slap of paint or wallpaper will make an immediate impact. Then clothe the walls with things you like to look at: pictures, paintings, prints, mirrors, hats and bags, even bicycles. The things you use every day can be very decorative.

If the space is large enough for storage, put up shelves (they can be freestanding) or a corner unit of cupboards. If storage is a problem in the rest of the house, then cupboards are much to be recommended. Low worktop-height cupboards can be used as working space, doubling up for model making, stamp collecting, homework and ironing, and for storing some of the things there's never been a right place for, such as shoes.

Tall, narrow cupboards can be used to hold tennis rackets and hockey sticks should you be a sports freak. Most households have a number of awkwardly shaped items for which there is no room in the hall and which clutter up the place, no matter how they are moved around from wardrobe top to under the bed in an effort to find homes for them.

A more drastic solution, in terms of the money you would have to spend, is to turn this space into a shower cubicle. You'd have to get your landlord's permission and check the building regulations. The best thing would be to get a professional to come and advise, install and deal with the permissions necessary.

If your front door is on a landing, you could put an old-fashioned

Above & left: A neglected and damaged fireplace can be transformed from eyesore to eyecatcher if painted an unexpected sugar almond colour and used as a frame for plants.

umbrella stand there and some pegs so that you and your visitors can park belongings outside instead of having to bring everything indoors. You'd have to feel fairly safe about intruders and burglars to do this, though.

If you had the money, you could probably box in the landing and hang a door which would give you a little extra privacy and fewer draughts. You could then set it up as a little workroom where a chest of drawers could hold materials and wall storage could hold most of the tools of your trade. The trick of covering a wall with cork or pinboard could be tremendously useful here.

Fireplaces

Many old houses have enormous fireplaces in their living-rooms and these are normally so decorative in themselves that they should be used as a centre of attention even if you never intend to light a fire there. Georgian ones will have generous mantelshelves and fine proportions and are often made of rather splendid materials, such as marble. Obviously since you can't and wouldn't want to ignore such splendour, it's sensible to make something of the fireplace, even if it's not used for fires. Fill the grate with flowers (fresh and dried) or plants instead of flame, or put a gas or electric fire in the grate. The shelf should not be used for miscellaneous papers if you can help it, but for the arrangement of objects which you cherish. The whole thing always looks good with a large mirror above it. Don't necessarily go for symmetry on your shelf. A balance of objects, perhaps boxes, a candlestick or two, some figures or collections of glasses, pottery, or Victoriana can all look interesting. The Victorians were inclined to build smaller fireplaces, though more ornate. You will find fireplaces with tiled surrounds, or all metal ones, which respond well to a coat of blacking and a polish.

In the fifties, fireplaces became more mundane with rectangular surrounds and these are often now fitted with gas or electric fires. You can forget tradition with these and cover their square and rather dull proportions with spectacular abstract designs of your own devising or with polka dots or contrasting primary colours. Very often they look best painted one colour, say red, and act as a backcloth for the television.

Tiles look good in juxtaposition to a fireplace and particularly on the hearth. If you collect tiles, or can only afford to buy a few at a time, place them on the floor in front of the fire, don't fix them permanently. A couple of rows will look picturesque, prevent cinders spoiling the carpet and can be taken away when you leave. If you don't intend to use the fireplace as a fireplace, make sure the flue is blocked to stop draughts. A bit of cardboard wedged inside the chimney should do the trick. Alternatively, you can fix a sheet of hardboard at the back. If you are going to use it, make sure you get the chimney swept regularly and find an attractive fireguard. Second-hand brass and velvet settles are good for sitting on and tall mesh guards should be used to keep children at bay. Both kinds at the very least will prevent pieces of hot coal falling on to the carpet.

Big baskets look fine next to a traditional fireplace and can be filled with logs, if you burn them, or with plants, dried flowers or even patchwork pieces.

Another source of heating you may well find is an electric fire simply stuck on to the wall, like a wart, usually at about waist height. They leave the feet cold and look very bleak but they can be cheered up. Put a rug under the fire to comfort the toes. Then collect some little objects to sit on the fireplace: a collection of tiny pebbles, a vase of dried grasses and put something really eyecatching on the wall above – a Chinese kite, an enormous poster, a collection of silver jewellery in a row on pins stuck into the wall, for instance, or a collection of fans. Fix them securely so they won't slip off into the fire. (Modern fires must have fireguards fixed to them by law, but it's better to be safe then burned.)

Windows

Window treatments should either provide a frame for a pleasant view, give privacy for the people inside and/or contribute to the decorative scheme. But no two windows, it seems, are the same size, shape, height or width. In converted houses a window may actually have been divided in half so you're getting half the amount of light, and that from a window squeezed up against a corner, so that it is less efficient and looks peculiar. For every window there is a solution, even if it means giving the thing up as as source of light and simply using it as a 'decorative feature'.

Small windows
Very small windows are always difficult to deal with. They don't bring in much light and they don't do much for the proportions of a room. You can ignore them and avoid drawing attention to them by not curtaining them. High up windows on stairs, landings or in lavatories hardly impinge on the consciousness anyway and can be safely left alone since it's hardly likely anyone will be trying to peep through them. Alternatively, you can go to the opposite extreme, paint the window as though it was indeed a picture. Small windows near the ceiling of a basement room will look good with short, brightly coloured or patterned curtains which can have inverted scallops at the top and be hung like café curtains.

Bow windows
These usually look best with several narrow curtains pulled together at night. If the window is ugly, draw a curtain right across and don't try to follow the window line with it.

Odd windows
If you have two windows of different sizes set in the same wall, you can conceal their differences by the furniture you use, putting a chair in front of one and not the other, building up storage boxes in front of both, drawing sheer curtains right down to ground level over the whole wall, putting up judicious shelving and so on.

The red velvet curtain is purely decorative, framed by the simple arch of the window and itself acting as a frame for the plants and sculpture on the sill.

Offset windows

A smallish window which is not quite in the centre of the wall, typical of back rooms in Victorian houses can be dealt with in two ways: you can fit a bookcase at each side with a window seat between them. You can cover the blank wall area with a louvred shutter which makes the window look twice its size. You could use mirror tiles with a painted frame round to give a similar but more dramatic effect. If the window is rather high up, you can fit bookshelves all round it with a window seat underneath it. A roller blind would finish this scheme off very well. You could do this in a Regency stripe, in Laura Ashley posies or in bold, modern fabrics and each would look completely different.

Deceiving the eye

To make a window seem wider than it is, put up a rod wider than the window and hang opaque curtains on it. When you draw the curtains, pull them only as far as the window frame which will suggest that the window extends farther than it actually does. Similarly, if a window is a bit squat for the room, you can make it seem taller by fixing the rod higher than the frame and covering the space with a valance or cornice.

6· Colour, pattern and style

Colour

What are the rules?

Colours affect human moods and feelings to a remarkable extent. Theoretically, red is understood to be a stimulating colour, yellow is 'sunny' and brightens the mood, blue is supposed to be cool and calm, purple regal, black sultry and so on. You can probably recognize the truth of this from your own experiences and feelings about particular colours. But different people do react differently to colour and rules are being broken all the time. So be aware of these psychological definitions, but follow your own instincts. The more you experiment, the more you'll learn and practising is fun and stimulating, though you must watch that experimenting doesn't become too expensive.

There are more colours and tones of colour than it's conceivable to imagine. For example there's no such colour as plain brown: there are soft, warm browns, cow pat browns, continental coffee, peat, stripped pine, mahogany, boot polish browns and browns that veer towards burgundy or dead grass. Each looks different, produces a different mood and reacts differently with other colours.

This is equally true of yellow, which gives you primrose, egg-yolk, citrus, unripe lemon, the browny yellow of hay, orangey yellows and canary yellows. Get your eye in by looking, noting and comparing manufacturers' shade cards. One colour might look quite yellow next to green, but might itself look green next to orange. The same applies to blues, greens and reds. Even white is by no means always the same colour and there are many different blacks.

There are really two ways to tackle the colour scheme. The first is to follow certain understood rules or guidelines and the second is to break the rules, experiment, choose colours you want whether they are 'suitable' or not and be prepared to change them if they don't work. If in doubt, follow the rules until you feel more confident. The basic rules run more or less like this:

1. Choose a main colour and follow it throughout your room, house or flat – whatever you have. White is safe but a bit hard to live up to. It looks warmer to paint the walls soft colours, such as magnolia,

which has a pinkish tinge, or muffin, a warm beigy colour, or a cooler grey. Grey, however, does need a disciplined design.

2. Paint the woodwork, including window and door frames, white.

3. Choose a secondary colour for floors, ceilings and so on, which will complement your main colour.

Colours which you might like to try together are brown/beige, deep blue/pale blue, yellow/grey, mahogany/pink, apricot/stone and deep green/sand. Or, rather than follow my ideas, think of flowers or any natural thing whose colours seem to you to go well together and use those. It's useful to get a box of paints or some scraps of fabric and experiment with colour combinations. If in doubt, woodwork nearly always looks best painted white.

If you follow these rules you will have an excellent basis on which to add patches of bright colour like reds, yellows, blues and greens, in the form of curtains, blinds, upholstery, cushions and so on.

If you feel you want to be a little more adventurous, be brave. A room painted entirely in deep blue with white or grey woodwork is easier to live with than a mish mash of 'safer' colours put together without rhyme or reason. Decide on a colour, stick to it and carry it through. Personal taste is terribly important – *you* have to live in the place, after all. But there is no doubt that colours go in fashion just as clothes do. During the early sixties the fashionable colours were orange and olive, and it was considered very advanced to paint a room one colour on three walls and orange or olive on the fourth. The sixties also brought stick-at-nothing swirls of every colour under the sun. The reaction in the seventies was chocolate brown. In the eighties, grey has become the fashionable main colour, but there are also fashions for pastel blues, greens and pinks, uninhibited primary colours, sometimes used together to create a rich patchwork in an otherwise ugly and inconvenient room. If deep colours are what you like, carry the main colour over walls and carpeting everywhere from hallway to bathroom. Use it plain in paint, or patterned on wallpaper and fabric, but stick to it.

One problem of choosing colours is that colour charts for paints offer such a mass of choice it's difficult to get a colour on its own and see what it really looks like. Another problem is that colours change depending on the size of area they cover, the way the light shines on them, the texture of the material (whether shiny or matt, rough or smooth, wool or nylon) and according to the colours placed near them. Years of experience have taught professional interior decorators to know what will happen to certain colours in certain situations, but it's hard for the beginner. Colours which look pale on the paint chart, may turn out to be darker and quite ugly when seen on their own. It's usually safe to go for colours you like to wear and a look at your own wardrobe will often give useful hints (though not always). Unexpected things happen in different lights and different situations so listen to your instincts, but try to check up before committing yourself to masses of wallpaper and paint. Some manufacturers sell small tester pots so you can paint a section of the wall to see what it will really look like before committing yourself to the whole lot.

Using colour to camouflage

Colours can be manipulated; you are not at their mercy. Very light rooms can be decorated in cool colours, since the daylight coming though windows will automatically bring the colour to life.

Gloomy rooms, where the daylight is excluded by trees or the buildings opposite can be decorated in pale and bright colours; yellow and green, if chosen well, often manage to produce a lighter feeling. Remember, mirrors will help to double any natural light if they face a window, and will double the amount of colour you have chosen too. Cold rooms, particularly basements with their suggestion of damp, can be given an added warmth by using reds and oranges.

Vertical stripes can make a room look taller but narrower. They also have an aura of Regency and stateliness so take care in a small Victorian or modern room, that you do not give a mistaken impression of the room being too big for its boots.

Vertical stripes are probably best applied as wallpaper though one young friend of mine striped one wall with green insulating tape which was remarkably effective. You'd probably need somebody to hold one end while applying the tape.

Horizontal stripes can make a room look wider but lower, which may be a good thing in great big Victorian rooms where the height dwarfs furniture and people and is difficult to make cosy. You can draw horizontal stripes freehand, perhaps deliberately introducing a slight wave or difference in height here and there, or use a tape measure to get them absolutely straight. Screen the outsides of your line with masking tape to get a clean finish.

Small-patterned wallpapers can make a room look larger and can certainly hide defects in the wall finish. They look pretty and fresh and will not detract from pictures you want to hang on the wall. As for using large patterned designs – look out! They are more difficult to get right, and can positively overwhelm a small room making it look even smaller. What's more, large patterns usually dominate any pictures or objects hung on them for decoration. Wallpapers with large designs are more difficult to hang too because the pattern must match and this isn't always easy to do. You may need an extra roll.

While you are pondering the choice of paints and papers, look and look and look: in shop windows, in magazines and in other people's homes. It's not so much a question of copying, though there's nothing wrong with using good ideas in your own way, but more of getting your eye in. Decorating is like reading – it doesn't come automatically (except to a few people) – you have to practise it.

Subdued backgrounds

You may choose to have a subdued background for several reasons. Perhaps you simply like traditional decoration, or feel that the proportions of the room merit the traditional. Perhaps you have many belongings and feel that they in themselves are so 'busy' that they need 'quiet' surroundings.

The beige, pastel or grey shades I mentioned earlier will probably be best as basic colour. Brown can be pleasantly 'enclosing' but don't use it in very dark rooms. You will probably find the shades of

Deep blue and pale blue have been used here to create a simple, comfortable room of casual elegance. The material of the blinds echoes the trellis pattern on the walls.

Right: A very simple stencil is not difficult to design and can be used as a wall frieze, floor decoration, on beams or furniture.

Above: *The pleasant proportions of this yellow room are accentuated by the white cornice and darker mustard of the ceiling. The attractive ceiling rose is also painted white.*

Left: *Thin green stripes made of sticky tape, cheap pine shelves from the local DIY store and a bright red fan make a Chinese corner in this tiny apartment.*

creamy coffee are easier to live with than the shades of horse-dropping brown. Window and door frames, skirtings and architraves should be painted white which will accentuate good woodwork and highlight the colour of the walls. Another good colour is apricot, but don't get it too pink. The basic background colour can be altered radically by the colours you add to it. Yellows, blues, greens, reds and browns will all blend in well.

If you'd rather go pastel, take care not to be too insipid. The sort of pastels in favour at the moment are quite sharp pinks and greens, not traditional bathroom tile colours, but shades of sugared almonds and liquorice allsorts – something you can get your teeth into! This sort of thinking is not afraid of bright baby blue walls for a kitchen or bathroom or, as I've seen it in a television room (what Americans would call the 'media room') with bright pink skirtings and window frames. The success of this scheme is in its simplicity; the room is just big enough to hold a television set on a table and a three-seater sofa. So, you see, pastel colours may sound a bit prissy and more appropriate to babies, but they don't have to be.

Bright paints are only one way of adding colour to a room. Lampshades, tablecloths, fruit, flowers, objects, wall hangings, brightly coloured storage units, painted furniture and upholstery can all add colour. In a flat I know which is shared by three young men are individual shelves set into the wall at angles and painted pink, green and blue respectively. They are ornaments in themselves and break away from those purely functional shelving systems which have been so popular for two decades.

Really deep colours are exciting to use. They do an excellent job as camouflage and can be used to great effect in tall, narrow and cold Victorian lavatories with uneven floors and pipes all over the place. If you paint the walls, say dark blue, the pipes and cistern red, the floor green and the lavatory seat yellow, you will create a work of art instead of a plumbing disaster.

Pattern

Most homes have too many patterns vying with one another. Pattern, after all, is provided by everything in the room – furniture, books, pictures, papers, objects and so on. But pattern specifically on walls and floors can be judiciously added to the overall scheme of things and be useful in covering up eyesores.

Pattern from paint

Painting is one of the easiest decorating jobs once you have prepared the surfaces properly. To add pattern with paint is easy too and there's no need to go in for sophisticated stippling or marbling techniques. You can get a decorative and interesting effect simply by using a large round or square-ended sponge, dipping it in contrasting paint and dabbing it over the walls at fairly regular intervals. This is an effective way of making painted walls a little more interesting, covers up blemishes and is very much cheaper than buying wall-paper. You could use the sponging technique on existing paint (provided it's in good condition), which would be even cheaper still. Very little paint is needed for this technique.

If you don't fancy an overall pattern you can add a bit of interest by painting two or three stripes horizontally all round a wall. A wide band of contrasting colour or two or three toning bands about two-thirds of the way up can look very effective in a tall room. Alternatively, paint the stripes one-third of the way up the wall and carry them round or over the door itself. Or cover the door with a simple painting or a *trompe-l'oeil* picture.

A cheap, effective and highly personal way to put pattern into your dump and cover up blemishes is with stencils. There are kits available of simple stencil designs (see address section) and armed with these and a can of aerosol paint you can create wonderful effects, not just on walls and floors, but on cupboards, curtains, cushions and so on. For a very small outlay you can transform a room and have a good deal of control over the result.

If you want to make your own stencils, you can cut out designs (preferably in parchment, but thin card will do) and paint over the cut out parts with a stiff-bristled brush.

Patterns from wallpaper and fabric

If you hanker after the neat and pretty, there are innumerable wallpapers available that are bright, fresh and inexpensive. This is an influence started by Laura Ashley, in whose shops you will still find some of the most inventive and cheapest of wallcoverings.

There are, of course, many cheap alternatives. Wrapping paper or old wallpaper samples can be used to make a patchwork wall and I have heard of a living-room in which one wall was entirely covered in cooking foil which helped to keep the heat in, but looked spectacular for only a short time. Collages are a constant source of pleasure and amusement and can be used to cover walls in bathrooms, lavatories, long passages or children's rooms.

The Americans are very talented at combining patterns. They are able to put different floral designs next to and on top of each other and still keep an overall sense of unity, but it's difficult to do this without producing something overbearing or prissy. Many chain stores and department stores now sell ranges of wallpapers with matching or toning fabrics using the same design in different forms, or plain colours to match designs which can be used together to make elegant interiors. However, they can be a bit limiting if taken too seriously because all the furniture and accessories will have to be in keeping or the effect will be wasted.

Matching fabrics and wallcoverings are useful in very small rooms and need not be too 'busy'. Staircase walls and landings benefit from the consistent use of one colour or pattern throughout to make them less 'bitty' and more part of a harmonious whole.

Floor patterns

Pattern need not be confined to walls and curtains. Patterned floors are popular and are supposed not to show the dirt, but a dirty floor will show through anything, believe me! You can add pattern to a plain floor by using huge floor cushions covered in exotic fabrics,

Above: *The colours in this room are reminiscent of a windswept moor, but a cosy effect is created with furnishings and objects in sympathetic colours. Although the windows are small, the light is maximized by using sheer curtains.*

Right: *This hand-painted jungle on a wall has a live plant in front to add depth. The birds were cut out of magazines and can be moved around. The effect is colourful and dramatic, doing away with the need for smart furniture and accessories.*

Above & left: *A sleazy bedroom has been transformed with a coat of paint and a brightly sponged finish. This effect is quickly and cheaply achieved, as one small pot of paint is enough for the second colour.*

Left: *A striking and deceptively simple wallpainting in an otherwise plain room adds interest and relieves the monotony of the woodchip wallpaper.*

patterned dhurries and kelims or colourful possessions, such as china, plants and baskets. Coordinating blinds and curtains will add interest and cohesion.

Tiles

Patterned tiles are useful behind a stove, a sink or a washbasin where the wall gets most greasy or splashed. They are easy to clean, don't cost much and you can make use of the pattern without dominating the room.

Style

Every house has its own style. The Georgians built in beautiful classic proportions for themselves and furnished grandly; for their servants they built minute cottages furnished sparsely with very simple objects. The Victorians built in a grandiose style, heavily furnishing their own floors, but putting their servants in basements or garrets, furnished very plainly. They also built tiny terraced back-to-back houses with no view and little garden. Each has its charm, though it's sometimes difficult to see when you first move in, and in particular, each has its personality.

Recognizing style

To a certain extent, a building should be paid the compliment of recognizing its personality and complementing it with appropriate decoration. This doesn't mean to say you must have Regency stripes in a Regency house, but a well-proportioned room will repay thoughtful decorating. Small attic bedrooms will look foolish if you try to pretend they are Georgian boudoirs and art deco is at its best in square, uncompromising modern rooms rather than in gracious, tall apartments with moulded ceilings. It's a question of recognizing and respecting the character and history of a building.

Of course many houses are now being divided into separate flats or bedsits and many rooms within such houses are being divided too, consequently losing some of their personality, some of their light (if they've lost a window) and some of their pleasing proportions. In these circumstances you have to use ingenuity to try to regain some of their original charm or change the character of the room.

Creating your own colour scheme

An excellent way of sorting out an idea is to make up a collection of paints, wallpapers, fabrics and floorings and then to experiment with different combinations of these until you get a scheme you like. This is great fun and also enormously helpful in sorting out ideas and establishing colour preferences. Choose the basic colours for the largest areas first and then add the rest. Find a piece of hardboard or card and pin small pieces of your samples on it. (Make sure they're big enough to see the patterns and textures. You can rearrange the pieces as often as you like, but the basic colour must dominate so you get the proportions right. It's best, as I've said earlier, to choose one basic colour, one secondary colour, which either contrasts or matches, and add 'dabs' of colour to these.

If you can't get samples of the real thing, piece your scheme together using bits of fabric, paper, ribbon, foil or anything begged, borrowed or found and when your scheme is decided, match them up carefully with the real thing in the shops. A sanded and sealed floor, for instance, if that's what you intend to have, can be simulated by wood grain paper, which won't be exactly right but will give you an idea. Look at the colours on the board in natural light and in artificial light and do the same when actually purchasing the materials.

Practical considerations

Use a matt paint for the walls and a gloss for the woodwork. Most paints are washable nowadays so you don't need to paint the kitchen in scrubbable white gloss in order to be able to get the cooking grease off the walls. Choose a water-soluble paint which will be easy to put on, dry fast and won't show lap or brush marks. These paints hardly smell at all. Splatters of paint can be wiped off quickly with a damp cloth, and brushes and rollers cleaned with soap and water while still wet. Don't let the paint dry and then try to clean it off – it's impossible.

When buying paint do buy enough. You can always use any extra for touching up, whereas if you run out before you've finished, you probably won't be able to match up the colour exactly with the original. The same is true of wallpapers and other wallcoverings. Get a roll too many rather than a roll too few. (Shops will usually take back unused rolls, but ask first.) Remember that pale colours painted over a dark wall will need more coats and that certain colours, such as red and yellow are particularly difficult to get right because of the way they react to light and other colours.

How much is enough? Measure the room carefully including the insides of cupboards and write down the measurements. Measure the height and·width of each wall and multiply to get the square area of that wall. Add up all the wall measurements for the total area. Then measure the window areas and subtract that total from your wall area.

The amount of paint you need will depend on how porous the wall surface is, the type and brand of paint and how many coats you need to apply. Usually there will be an indication on the tin or the manufacturer's leaflet, but here's a rough idea of what you can expect.

Oil or resin-based paint (thinned with white spirit)
liquid paint – 1 pint (0.5 lit) should cover 100 sq ft (9 sq m)
jelly paint – 1 pint (0.5 lit) should cover 75 sq ft (7 sq m)
Emulsion paint (water-based and available in matt or silk finish)
liquid paint – 1 pint (0.5 lit) should cover 90 sq ft (8 sq m)
jelly paint – 1 pint (0.5 lit) should cover 55 sq ft (5 sq m)

Acrylic or semi-gloss paint (water-thinned and available in semi-gloss or matt finish)
liquid paint – 1 pint (0.5 lit) covers 80–85 sq ft (7–8 sq m)
jelly paint – 1 pint (0.5 lit) covers 45–55 sq ft (4–5 sq m)

Polyurethane paint (forms a hard surface that is good for radiators and is available in gloss, semi-gloss and matt finish
jelly paint – 1 pint (0.5 lit) covers 75–100 sq ft (7–9 sq m)

A standard roll of wallpaper is 11 yards (10 m) long and 20½ inches (52 cm) wide. For a room of average height this will divide into four matching lengths, unless you've chosen a very large pattern. Check the height of your room between skirting and cornice and the length of the walls. The following ready reckoner chart will help you in your calculations.

HEIGHT OF ROOM		DISTANCE ROUND ROOM (including doors, windows, etc.)															
		ft	44	48	52	56	60	64	68	72	76	80	84	88	92	96	100
		m	13	14	15	17	18	19	20	21	23	24	25	26	28	29	30
ft	m							rolls of paper									
7	2.1		6	6	7	7	8	8	9	9	9	10	10	11	11	12	12
7½	2.3		6	6	7	8	8	9	9	10	10	11	11	12	12	13	13
8	2.4		6	7	7	8	8	9	9	10	10	11	12	13	13	13	14
8½	2.5		6	7	8	8	9	9	10	11	11	12	12	13	13	14	14
9	2.7		7	7	8	9	9	10	10	11	12	12	13	13	14	15	15
9½	2.9		7	8	9	9	10	10	11	12	12	13	14	14	15	15	16
10	3.0		8	8	9	10	10	11	12	12	13	14	14	15	16	16	17
10½	3.2		8	9	9	10	11	11	12	13	13	14	15	16	16	17	18
11	3.3		8	9	10	10	11	12	13	13	14	15	16	16	17	18	18

A colour board is useful for working out textures and colour before you go ahead and buy. It's an excellent way to get your eye in and to see what goes together.

Above: *The furniture in this sunny little room is very simple. The interest is provided by a number of pale but compatible colours and a variety of small but similar prints.*

Left: *A collection of second-hand Victorian tiles acts as a splashback and complements not only the small-patterned wallpaper, but the two prints as well.*

7 · Storage

Look at any home and you will see that storage is one of the most difficult things to organize properly. The most carefully planned interiors are cluttered up with the detritus of everyday living. Anything from teddy bears to old newspapers and cardboard boxes, bits of fabric, chipped cups and writing materials, all lie about waiting to be used or thrown away. You don't have to be obsessive about tidiness to feel that things which are properly stored look better, keep better and leave more room for action than a chaotic jumble.

Good storage means you have a place for everything. It makes things easy to find, easy to reach, easy to use and, if it's not enclosed, it's good to look at as well. It's definitely not just a chest of drawers in the bedroom or a box under the bed for throwing old shoes into. Pictures, for instance should be hung on walls under a good light where they can be seen; records are most conveniently kept upright, on shelves or in a cabinet. Books, papers, kitchen equipment, clothes, jewellery, 'collections', work materials, toys and tools all have to be stored somewhere, so storage must be well thought out, particularly in small spaces where it's necessary to find room for a lot of unrelated bits and pieces.

Some people feel more secure when surrounded by belongings; for instance, a student I knew in London had a room that was so full of clothes, cardboard boxes and other things that she had to work little passages through it which led to 'nests' of space, like a rabbit warren.

Most of us prefer our chaos to be more ordered and that means well-planned storage and plenty of it. The first thing is to list everything you own (or want to own), decide how often an item will be used and settle on a convenient place and what form of storage to use for it.

An assessment of what storage exists and how you can best use it will help you to plan what you need to add to it (or remove from it). Many houses have built-in cupboards and alcoves which can be used very conveniently with an added shelf or two for sound equipment, for instance. Though in some cases you might do well to tear out certain existing cupboards – those at temple height in a kitchen for instance, whose open doors could nastily knock you on the forehead, or cupboards riddled with rot, inconvenient shelves or so cramped that you can't fully open the doors or drawers. Sometimes a useless piece of storage can be moved into the bathroom and become quite useful for holding lavatory rolls and bleach.

Each room has its own particular function and the storage needs can be fairly easily worked out if you list the items that need to be stored in each place and then turn your mind round ways of storing them.

Planning

Work logically, room by room, and try to put everything in as convenient a place as possible.

Kitchens

Food should be stored near the sink or cooker. Pans should also be kept near the cooker, stacked on a shelf or hanging from hooks on the wall or ceiling. If you have enough floor space, a pyramid-shaped pan rack may be the answer.

Cleaning equipment should be stored out of reach of children, which usually means on a fairly high shelf, but where it can be kept tidy and ordered. If you don't have children to consider, you can safely store these things under the sink. Brooms and vacuum cleaners can be kept under the stairs if there's room to stand them upright, and it would be better still if they could be hung on the wall. You should use strong hooks or brackets for this and make sure you plug the wall.

Magazine storage
I This pocket needs stiff canvas and thick thread. The measurements on the diagram are a guide only. For greater accuracy, measure the armchair you want the pocket to fit, allowing about 9 inches (23 cm) for the actual pocket and hem.
2 Make a small hem to stop the pocket opening fraying. Sew the side seams of the pocket.
3 Position the pocket on the chair as shown. The part under the seat may be weighted with a piece of bamboo or a flat piece of metal stitched into a seam.

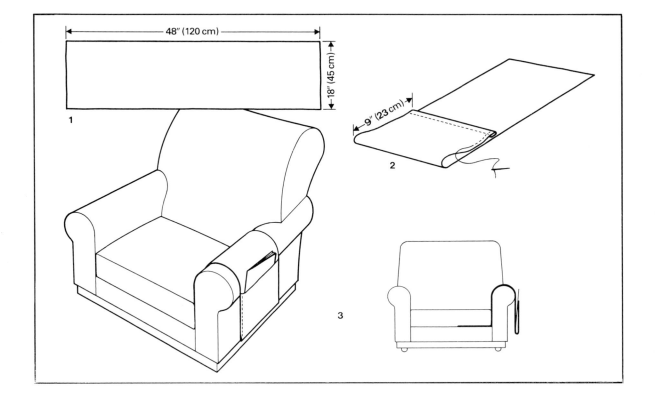

The clutter of food, jars and utensils in the tiny kitchen (below) makes it uncomfortable and inefficient to work in. Good storage is essential for hygiene and orderliness. The swivel shelving in the right-hand kitchen is inexpensive, keeps things tidy and makes them easy to find.

Opposite: A simple shelving system used neatly and to good effect. The small spotlamp fixes to the upright and a bracket is used to hold the books in place.

One very narrow shelf running round the kitchen, or along the kitchen wall of a bedsit, will take herb and spice jars, sauce bottles, salt and pepper shakers, and all the little things which so often get lost behind large packets in a cupboard. You will also need a shelf for cookery books, and this could be a good place to keep box files for correspondence and receipts.

Brackets for spices can be fixed to the inside of cupboard doors, and can be used also for baking equipment, cream of tartar, bicarbonate of soda, birthday candles, hundreds and thousands and little bottles of colouring.

Large jars and mugs are immensely useful; they can hold wooden spoons, fish slices, washing-up brushes, pens and pencils and paint or pastry brushes. A wine rack is useful for bottles, though there can't be many of us who manage to keep it full of wine! The empty holes are handy for rolls of aluminium foil, cling film and plastic bags, not to mention posters waiting to be framed or architects' plans of the house. Awkward items, like the iron or table mats, can be kept on top.

A plate rack is one of the best ways of drying and storing plates. They are available in wood or plastic at most department stores, and if you buy an upright one, it can be hung on the wall to save space.

Glass jars and metal boxes are good for storing dry food. Save your coffee jars and use them as canisters. You can see their contents and they can look very decorative if you store different coloured foods in them: brown sugar, black-eyed beans, orange and green lentils, rice,

preserved tomatoes and fruit can make your kitchen look like an expensive delicatessen.

Stemmed glasses can use up a lot of space, so take a lesson from pubs and hang them upside-down from slots cut into the edges of shelves. Take care that this idea doesn't render items below inaccessible.

Bathrooms

Bathroom storage is something few people take seriously. It usually consists of a small lockable cabinet for keeping medicines out of the reach of children, but this is not nearly enough. You will need to store towels, household and personal cleansers, mirrors, perhaps household linen and toys. Once you've made your list you can work out whether you want open or closed storage; do you want things to hang up, go in drawers, stack, range in rows or be relegated to high shelves where you needn't think of them again for ages?

A small second-hand pine cupboard which you can paint or strip would fit into most bathrooms and store quite a lot of things. If your bathroom is big enough, it would be best to have a built-in cupboard under the basin with a 'worktop' surround. Failing that, a set of shelves running up one wall and painted with gloss paint to protect against steam, could fill the storage gap.

Living-rooms

The living-room, as its name suggests, will house most of your possessions: books, records, pictures, sewing and writing equipment, stereo, television, tapes and bric-a-brac. Most of these things will be in regular use so open shelving is probably the best form of storage.

Try to get your books satisfactorily ranged on shelves as soon as you can. It's not good for them to be tightly squeezed into boxes. Shelves should have ends of some sort so the books are kept upright to protect their shape and bindings.

Magazines grow in number astonishingly fast and can take over the place unless you are strong-willed enough to throw them away. Give them to your dentist or local hospital. Copies of magazines you wish to keep for reference can be piled on deep shelves spine out, so you can read the name and date of each issue. Magazine racks tend to take up too much space for their usefulness. A canvas magazine-sized pocket slung over the arm of a chair is a Scandinavian solution which is easy to make (see page 73).

One really useful piece of office equipment which is ideal for home storage is the box file. These are fairly expensive to buy now, but can often be found second-hand and are perfect for photographs, bills, school information, brochures, guarantee leaflets and so on.

There are many small tool and nail boxes with clusters of small drawers to be found in DIY shops. These are useful for drawing pins, painting materials, woodwork tools and other small items it's hard to categorize.

Bedrooms

In the bedroom you will have to find hanging room for some clothes, shelf room for others, somewhere to put ties, shoes, belts, jewellery, hats and scarves – some of them quite awkward shapes which must be stored carefully and easily found again.

Bedsits

If you are not so lucky as to have four rooms, but are squeezing yourself and your possessions into a bedsit, your list is even more crucial and you may find you really need to cross some items off it altogether and throw them away.

The more you can hang up in a small space, the better: plate rack, cups, knife rack, oven gloves, saucepans and ironing board. This will leave more space on shelves and in cupboards. Try to get things that will stack, not just plates, but cups, storage jars, tins and so on. A set of tough brackets firmly fixed into the wall can provide a resting place for a cylinder vacuum cleaner. In fact with a bit of ingenuity and a strong set of wallplugs you can fix brackets on the wall for most cleaners. Your arrangements of brackets, shelves and hooks will depend on the particular cleaning equipment you own and the space available for it.

Choose chairs for sitting around or at table which will fold and tuck away behind the door. 'Director' style canvas chairs are ideal.

Choose a bed with drawers underneath, or with legs high enough to slide boxes beneath.

Order your cupboards by installing wire baskets, shelves and drawers so that you use the space to its fullest. Hang up pans on butchers' hooks hung over a bar fixed diagonally in the ceiling over the cooker. Once you have your list you can really start to 'think storage' and you will discover all sorts of solutions.

Types of storage can be categorized quite conveniently and the following list of different types of storage may make it easier to choose what you want.

Closed storage

Cupboards have the advantage of shutting in chaos. They also keep things relatively dust-free, which can be an advantage with some items. If your present dump is only temporary and you expect to move on soon, it would be sensible to concentrate on freestanding cupboards which you can take with you when you go. Old wardrobes can be stripped and sealed, painted or stencilled and you can still get good second-hand ones in plenty of junk shops. Find one that isn't too deep and measure the cupboard and the space it's to go in before you cart it home. Half an inch too big may not seem much, but it's too much. Beware – freestanding cupboards tend to dominate a room and usually take up more space than open shelves.

A cupboard is not just a cupboard. It's a space which you can use efficiently or you can waste; it all depends on how you plan it inside. For instance, a wardrobe might have a long shelf at the top, a hanging rail along half its length, a set of narrow shelves running up one side and a set of pockets.

Above: A piece of thirties Hollywood-style is used with great aplomb as a display cabinet. It needs a simple background.

A good layout for such a wardrobe might be:
1. Bags, luggage and blankets on the top shelf.
2. Hats, belts, socks and underwear on the narrow shelves.
3. Coats and suits or dresses hung at one end of the rail.
4. Short garments, such as shirts at the other end of the rail with the space below used for shelves or narrow drawers. Most department stores now sell modular units of wire baskets and drawers with runners which are quite inexpensive and organize the interior of a cupboard with great efficiency.

Far right: Another arrangement of cubes can act as room divider, display cabinet and storage. The pyramid shape makes it less of a barrier and more of a sculpture.

If you don't like or can't afford the ubiquitous kitchen 'unit', you could buy a small, old-fashioned wardrobe or a second-hand fifties kitchen cupboard-cum-dresser with slim metal or plastic handles, usually in pale eau-de-nil. These often have a flap-down cupboard

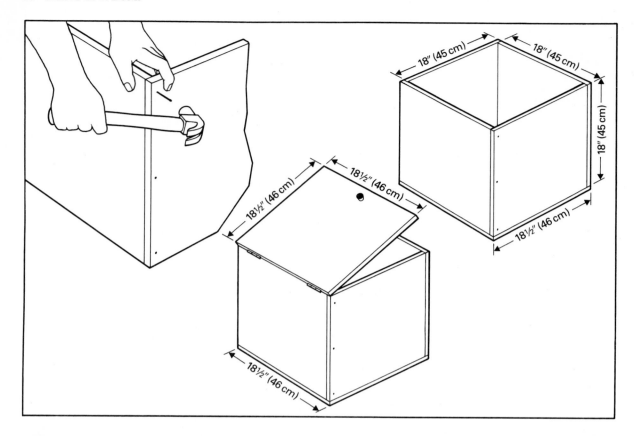

18" (45 cm)   18" (45 cm)
18" (45 cm)
18½" (46 cm)

18½" (46 cm)
18½" (46 cm)

18½" (46 cm)

Making a box

A box like this is not difficult to make. You could use chipboard or old shelves. Make sure the pieces are cut correctly and that the nails you use are thin and hammered in straight. The hinged square can be a lid or a door, depending on how much space you have to open it in.

door which can be used as a worktop, but you can remove this altogether if it gets in the way.

In fact, when buying second-hand you should think of the possibility of altering furniture to suit your needs. You can cut off legs to lower the height, or even slice something in half and use the two pieces separately. Dividing and altering offers much greater scope than sticking to the object as it stands.

Chests of drawers

Chests of drawers are always useful. They hold small fiddly things like underwear and socks, sweaters which should not be hung up, materials, papers, photography equipment, even tools – in fact, anything which looks untidy or may get damaged out in the open. They can be useful in a hall or on a landing, for gloves and dog leads, and in the kitchen for cutlery, linen, even saucepan lids. They are also useful for standing things on: vases of flowers, bowls of apples, the ironing and family photos.

Second-hand chests of drawers are available, at quite good prices, if you don't want mahogany or oak. New ones are usually made of pine and can be quite inexpensive, or of chipboard with a laminate finish, which is not wooden even if it tries to look like it. You'll find chests in a variety of shapes and sizes, but it's not always advisable to opt for the one which offers maximum space. Low chests of drawers between living-room seating units can solve a number of storage problems and be used as tables. They can even double as seating.

Boxes

Boxes must be among the oldest forms of furniture and have been used as seating, stacking storage, stepladders and goodness knows what else. Tea chests are often used to pack books, china and glass when moving house, and can be found in newspaper and magazine advertisements. Alternatively, banana boxes and apple boxes are very easy to get hold of. The boxes in which Indian crafts are packed and imported are often quite well made and you could be lucky enough to find one or two waiting to be thrown away outside the local gift shop.

Boxes which fit under the bed are useful for toys, blankets, duvets or pillows, especially in dual-purpose rooms. Drawers from a redundant chest of drawers are useful for this.

There are several versions of purpose-designed box storage, which stack on top of each other or sit side by side. These are not usually cheap but, like folding shelves, can be built up by degrees. Coloured plastic boxes are available from schools' suppliers, from places specializing in seconds and some children's toyshops.

Alternatively, you can make your own boxes. Ask your local timber merchant to cut four squares of ½ inch (1 cm) plywood or chipboard, say 18 inches (45 cm) square, plus one measuring 18½ inches (46 cm) square for the bottom. Glue or nail the sides together, placing the side of one board on the edge of the next, all round, so that the finished box measures 18½ inches (46 cm) square. If you want a lid or door, cut another square 17½ inches (44 cm) square and fix just inside the opening of the box, using concealed hinges on the right side and a cupboard catch on the left. Then screw in or glue on a knob.

Paint the finished box in gloss or polyurethane paint, allowing the exposed surfaces to dry before turning it over to do the others. If you prefer you can hire a staple gun and cover the whole box with fabric to match the curtains in the room. You can also make a matching cushion to go on top.

Range the boxes along a wall, stack them up, or use one on its own as a bedside table.

Open shelving

Shelving systems are the backbone of modern storage. There are various types on the market, mainly consisting of metal uprights with adjustable brackets, which support shelves made of wood, laminated chipboard or glass. Sometimes you can get cupboard units to use in conjunction with the shelves. This system has many advantages. You can make the shelves fit the alcove or a whole length of wall, corner-to-corner, it is relatively inexpensive, and you can add shelves or adjust the heights as you will.

Fitted shelving can go in all sorts of places, but alcoves and chimney breast recesses are obvious places. Since you are planning round your possessions, you can custom-make the shelves to fit the actual things you want to put in them. This eliminates gaps between the record shelf and the paperback shelf, and books of the same size can be stored together without wasting space.

Overleaf: *Although it looks expensive, the second-hand dresser was cheaper than the equivalent kitchen 'units', holds just as much equipment and looks prettier.*

Left: *An inspirational answer to storage by a girl who likes clothes. The two tier hanging rack is made of broomsticks and string; the cupboard is painted to match the carpet.*

Below: *This wall storage takes care of all sorts of awkward objects; it is easy to make a simple version yourself.*

Left: *A simple wire storage system fixed to the wall makes an exotic but practical place for beads, hats and glasses. The cork behind it is an excellent noticeboard and filing system.*

Above: *A set of wall pockets is a neat way to file gardening or sewing equipment. These are particularly good as they also have hooks and bulldog clips at the bottom.*

Above: *Poor storage makes it very difficult to be tidy and to use a space effectively. The cheap and ingenious hanging storage on the previous page puts this half-hearted attempt to shame.*

Deep shelves may hold a lot of items, but things become hidden and hard to reach. The storage ideas shown on the previous page cover most needs and ensure that everything comes easily to hand.

Shelving usually looks (and works) better if it has sides. This will be more expensive, but will stop books falling off the ends. A less likely, but valuable site for shelves would be a dark window, looking out, perhaps, on to a dustbin area where little light gets in and you don't specially want to see out. Glass shelves holding glass objects or wooden shelves holding plants will look decorative; the plants will benefit from the light and the glass will show up well with the light behind it.

If you want just an occasional shelf, individual brackets will be the most economical way of fixing. The cheapest (and probably the oldest) form of shelving is a bricks-and-plank arrangement. The main trouble with this is getting bricks which are equal in size so the shelves don't rock about, and carrying them any distance because they are bulky and heavy. You can buy bricks from a builders' merchant, but if you get your bricks from a skip, the chances of them matching are quite remote.

Chipboard or laminated chipboard will make satisfactory shelves, supported on bricks, though they need support at two-foot intervals if they are not to bow with weight. If you can get hold of some really thick planks of wood (try skips again) you could make a very stylish set of shelves indeed.

Metal office shelving can be obtained cheaply, but it is hardly cheerful. It is usually only available in gunmetal grey or filing-cabinet green, but you can always spray it with car-enamel paint which is available in superb colours. Second-hand office furniture suppliers will probably have such shelving or you may see it advertised in small ads in newspapers.

Unpainted wooden shelves which fold and stack can be found in DIY and decorating shops and some furniture stores. They are inexpensive, especially as you can build up your stock gradually, unit by unit. Eventually they can be used to cover a whole wall or ranged along a wall at waist height. One on its own can act as a telephone table. They are not the sturdiest pieces of furniture in the world, but are easy to carry and take away, look quite good and shoulder quite heavy loads if you set them up properly.

If you have decided on open shelving but you would like to cover up the contents sometimes, roller blinds can be used. Since you are trying to restore order from the chaos, I would suggest you use a deep, plain colour, and don't try to pretty up the situation with patterned fabric, which will be confusing to the eye.

Room dividers

There may be several reasons for dividing a room, but the bonus is that it can provide extra storage. A worktop-height divider opening on either side, is good for separating the kitchen and eating area. You can put the plates in one side after washing up and take them out the other for laying the table. A taller divider, in the form of shelves all the way up, or cupboards below and shelves above can be arranged in the same way, using the taller part for books, or plants or a permanent display of dishes or other objects.

Wire storage

Wire baskets are almost standard pieces of kitchen equipment. You can buy them from kitchen suppliers or improvise with wire filing trays from second-hand office furniture suppliers. They can be used on their own, simply sitting on shelves, or hooked underneath as drawers – very useful for things like cooking foil and dusters. Such baskets can also be stacked on top of each other using special clip-on struts, and make useful vegetable racks. In the bedroom, they make excellent storage for separating small items such as socks and scarves, and for keeping clean shirts folded and flat.

Wire mesh panels have recently appeared on the market, which can be fixed to the wall and used in conjunction with wire hooks to provide hanging storage. These can be very space-saving and convenient in kitchens for all the small gadgets which get shoved to the backs of drawers and lost among the muddle: corkscrews, sieves, tea strainers, measuring spoons, rolls of sticky tape and so on. In bedrooms, they provide an excellent way of storing jewellery, scarves, gloves and hats.

A cheaper alternative to these specially made panels and hooks is an inverted wire basket. You can fix it to the wall using cup hooks.

Slatted storage

Alf Martensson, who runs a kitchen design company, created this very simple hanging system, that looks good in any kitchen. It can take up as much or as little space as you like, is very easy to put up and takes care of storing lots of difficult bits and pieces, including even a framed print or two. With a bit of ingenious planning, this system can be made to look quite formal, and is always decorative as well as being highly practical.

To make your own, measure the height and width of the space you want to fill with slats. Cut two batons of $2 \times \frac{1}{2}$ inch (5×1 cm) wood to the length you require. Then cut several lengths of the same size wood to the width you require and nail them at half-inch (1 cm) intervals to the uprights. Fix this 'ladder' to the wall. Then make as many hooks as you like from old wire coat hangers using a pair of pliers.

Baskets

Baskets can make attractive miscellaneous storage and will always look good if you remember to dust or scrub them from time to time. Their natural colour is pleasant, but there's no reason why you shouldn't paint them any colour you like. If you want to make a basket less rustic, you can line it with a cotton fabric. As linen storage, log storage, sewing storage or out-of-season clothes storage, baskets are marvellous because they are highly decorative in their own right. A big laundry hamper looks wonderful in a simply furnished bedroom and will hold blankets, duvets, extra pillows or outgrown clothes.

Other ideas

So much for fundamental storage which will become part of the structure of your life. You will still be left with numerous bits and pieces which have no home, but there are plenty of ideas for these.

A young friend of mine, who has a passion for jumble sales and clothes in general, made herself a double hanging rail fixed in an alcove between one wall and a wardrobe. Each rail hangs from strings threaded through hooks screwed into the ceiling, but it is possible to get special little brackets for clothes rails. Long clothes, such as coats and dresses hang on the lower rail and above that she keeps blouses, shirts and tee-shirts. In this way she can house an enormous quantity of garments in a very small flat, without feeling squeezed out by her own clothes. Hanging storage is important. If you have no wardrobe and don't want to fix rails permanently, you can get metal rails on castors, of the sort used in some shops.

In hallways, Victorian mirrors incorporating narrow shelves and umbrella stand, can be used for coats and gloves. Search around in junk shops for such discarded gems.

Old-fashioned hat stands have become fashionable and hard to find, but you can buy new ones (rather expensively) in chain furniture stores. They can be an attractive way of storing hats, scarves, shirts, coats, jackets and jewellery, especially in bedsits where space is scarce.

Dressmaking models can often be found in junk shops and are useful for jewellery, too, though often more attractive to look at than practical to use, since necklaces are apt to get knotted together without some care. You can use these padded bodies as pincushions for brooches and badges, and they can be draped with scarves and shawls plus a hat or two.

Cork or pinboard on a wall makes a good basis for jewellery storage, especially if you like to see it used to decorative effect, rather than hiding it away in jewellery caskets.

Canvas pockets are useful for miscellaneous objects like seed packets, markers, labels, slug killer, pens and pencils, rubbers and paper clips. You can sometimes find this sort of storage in department stores or charity shops, but you can easily make your own if you have a sewing machine. Batons of wood slipped into the top and bottom hems help it to retain its shape.

Shelves can be edged with strong carpet binding, tacked firmly at intervals leaving gaps wide enough to slot in pairs of scissors, balls of string and pens. Cup hooks screwed under or into the fronts of shelves will store not just cups but mugs, jugs and anything with a handle or loop.

Second-hand office furniture can be gratifyingly cheap and useful. Box files are excellent for storing paperwork and photographs. Desks, filing cabinets, metal shelving and all kinds of office furniture can be efficient and useful. Typists chairs are good if you work at home since they are ergonomically designed for comfort and support, and can be adjusted to suit your height and that of the desk.

It is well worth buying a set of good kitchen knives, but you should take great care of them. Store them safely in a rack where they won't

Far right: With a lot of self-discipline, a few shelves, a table-top desk and some filing cabinets, it's possible to squeeze an effective little workspace into a cupboard.

damage or get damaged by other items in a drawer. Magnetic racks are available, but racks with slots are safer. You can make your own slots in the back of a draining board (check with your landlord first) or you can buy a freestanding knife block with different sized slots, or get one that will fix to the wall.

If you have a large cupboard, it's tempting to make it a dumping ground. However, much more useful would be to make your own study inside which you can shut away when you are not working. Fitted shelves will hold most of the equipment and one wide shelf at worktop height can be your desk. Pinboard at one side or at the back will hold lists and reminders. Baskets on the floor can hold materials and there may be room for a sewing machine. Shelves fixed above doors can hold filing boxes and reference books.

8·Furniture and lighting

Furniture

Different people find different ways of providing themselves with furnished comfort in cramped quarters. Sailors used to sleep in hammocks, the Russian peasant family on top of the warm stove, the Japanese rolled up their bedding during the day and the Shakers hung their furniture on the wall to get it out of the way.

As accommodation has become scarcer, and therefore smaller, these ideas have begun to make sense again and there are now many ingenious methods of using space to its best advantage and of designing furniture which is neat, good-looking and useful.

Most people have more furniture than they actually need and many places would be much more comfortable if the furniture were confined to a bed, a couple of chairs and a table, without the inevitable three-piece suite and 'occasional' tables. It's better to start off with too little and build up gradually than to stuff an apartment full of kind offerings which someone else doesn't want, or with pieces bought simply because they were dirt cheap.

A mattress on the floor and a few hooks on a wall will be quite adequate to see you through the painting and decorating stages by which time you will have a better idea of how you'd really like to arrange the place. Vigorously resist the temptation to accept offers of ropey old sofas with the springs scraping the floor and miscellaneous tables, chairs, wardrobes and tallboys which will take up space without giving satisfaction.

I shall concentrate, in this chapter, on furniture which will use a small space economically but will be comfortable and look good.

Searching around is part of the planning stage. Study pictures in books and magazines, other people's homes and room sets in stores. Latch on to ideas which please or excite you, consider them in the light of your own space and see if they'll 'go'. Measure your space and the furniture carefully. Check that what you are buying will not only get through the front door and up the stairs, but that there will be enough space for doors and drawers to open fully and, in the case of seating, for people's knees when they are sitting down. You don't want your room to be like the inside of a jumbo jet where the tall have to sit with their knees under their chins or stretch their legs into the aisle.

Above: *This two-seater sofa in smart striped cover, doubles up as a bed for a bedsit dweller or for visitors.*

Right: *The Japanese solution, a Futon or bed roll, makes a comfortable mattress at night and folds or rolls into a sofa during the day.*

A folding chair with a sculptural look, designed and made in Denmark, has its own wooden wall bracket so it can be stored out of the way.

Below: An extremely neat trestle table which could be used permanently for working or eating or be folded away when not needed. The 'rise and fall' light adds versatility to this arrangement.

Beds

You spend nearly one-third of your life in bed, so you must look for something lasting and comfortable to sleep on. A bed that doesn't support the body properly will make you feel tired and give you back pain. In general a firm bed is better than a soft one. The only way to tell what suits you is to try it. Don't buy a second-hand mattress for a bed which is to be used regularly.

Anything that saves space is, on the face of it, a good idea. Dual-purpose furniture, such as a bed settee, can solve a lot of problems. If it's to be used every night, make sure it is going to be firm and give you proper support. Other ostensibly practical ideas like a bed which swivels to make a table, or a table you can use as an ironing board sound ideal, but can cause more problems than they're worth, particularly to the undisciplined. What's the betting you'd want to be eating your dinner while the bed is still rumpled and unmade, or to climb into bed while the table is still covered with some unresolved game of cards? Dual-purpose furniture can be a godsend, but it must be practical and simple; beware of the too clever.

Having said that, there's some very useful and cheap dual-purpose furniture about. Among the most practical is the bed settee which nowadays comes in so many shapes, forms and prices that you'll almost certainly find one to fit your situation. You can get fully-fledged sofas that pull out to make double or single beds, foam rectangles that fold over to become modular seating or Japanese futons, that are simply mattresses which can be rolled up and hidden during the day. Rather sophisticated versions are being made nowadays which can be half rolled up and used as sofas. Some have slatted bases which makes them look more like 'real' furniture.

An old solution to the bed-space problem is to have a hinged bed base with boxed-in sides, which folds back against the wall under a sort of mantelshelf. In Germany, where I first came across this idea, the enormous duvet was held in by a large strap. Versions of this are available in some shops nowadays. (Much more sophisticated versions can be found which pivot so that when the bed is to the front it can be pulled down, but at other times, faced the other way, a bookcase is revealed. The whole thing is recessed into the wall so you'd never guess there was a bed there at all.)

Two-tier or three-tier beds, are usually metal-framed and sprung, and might be a good answer to your own sleeping needs and for occasional overnight visitors, particularly for children who like to be able to ask friends to stay the night without too much notice. Bunk beds are obviously space-saving if you are sleeping more than one person in a smallish room. My sister once shared a London flat in which four girls slept in four bunk beds in one small room. But the idea can be extended to creating space for just one person by having a bed on top and storage or study space underneath, or vice versa.

Seating

Besides your bed or bed settee, you will need somewhere else for people to sit. Large floor cushions are useful, but they look best in rather bare rooms, otherwise they lie around like great whales and get in people's way. You can make your own very easily using curtain fabric or even dress material if it's not too flimsy. Fill them with chopped up old tights or foam bits, which you can often find in markets. You can use kapok, but it is heavy and bulky, liable to lump together and impossible to wash. Sack chairs (or sag bags) are easy to make. Fill them with round polystyrene granules that act like ball bearings and group to fit round you when you sit down, not odd broken bits which crunch together uncomfortably (see page 124 for suppliers).

Modular foam seating can be bought one piece at a time and put together in a variety of arrangements that give great flexibility to the layout of a room. Some systems are simply seating consisting of base and back; others have corner units and some of the units may have arms. Many open out so they can be slept on as well. Usually they have washable covers.

Upright seating is necessary if you want to eat comfortably. Moulded plastic stacking chairs with chrome legs are available from office suppliers in bright and pleasing colours.

Folding dining-chairs are a real blessing and most furniture shops stock various types. They are comparatively cheap and range from high-tech perforated metal to chrome and plastic, or pale wood with slatted or cane seats. They take up little space when folded but if they do get in the way, they can be hung up on the wall. They are easy to carry from room to room and if you choose carefully, are quite comfortable enough to sit on throughout a meal.

Traditional chairs with four legs should be chosen for their slimness if you want to seat lots of people round a dining table.

Tables

If you want to be able to eat in comfort you will have to have a table of some sort. Low tables are not ideal for eating at. A folding kitchen table, or 'bar' will do better than nothing while a card table can be used at a pinch. Covered with a pretty cloth (and yet another, smaller one on top) it won't be recognizable as a card table at all. (Get two if you want to seat more than two people.)

Trestles are useful because you can move them and stack them. The top can be a piece of laminated chipboard, thick glass or a door. If you want to get rid of the table you can store the trestles and the top under the stairs or in a broom cupboard. Extending tables are useful, particularly if the extension is easy to manipulate. Folding decorators' tables are inexpensive and can be painted or covered in fabric.

Trolleys can be used to store objects as well as for transporting them; a row of trolleys could make movable storage for a number of things, such as drinks, plates, 'home office' papers or even toys.

Second-hand

In my opinion it's better to buy something well made and well designed which has been used before, than something new and shoddy which nobody will ever want to use again. There's plenty of well built second-hand furniture to be found in junk shops, in spite of the fact that second-hand has become fashionable and lots of people are looking for the same thing.

Avoid second-hand veneers, especially if you can see the surface beginning to peel away. Modern veneers are durable because glues have become so much better, but old ones are not so reliable. Victorian furniture is solid and often dark-stained, though nowadays it is often found stripped, which makes it blonde and good-looking but much more expensive. There's no reason why you shouldn't strip furniture yourself if you are prepared for the painstaking time and effort it will inevitably require. Use a proprietory stripper and a scraper followed by sandpaper and steel wool, and anything else you find convenient. It can be wonderfully satisfying to restore a decrepit piece of furniture to some of its former glory.

There are plenty of second-hand kitchen cupboards and units from the fifties, usually in cream or eau de nil with red plastic handles. These can give the kitchen a refreshingly different look from the dull uniform of badly-made fitted kitchen units since they are freestanding and rather more like furniture. However, they need thought and care to make them look their best, and merit a search around for accessories from the same period, such as enamelled tea and coffee tins.

A fifties cocktail cabinet (from a jumble sale) has had the legs cut off and is useful as a telephone table and display cabinet. Note the wall collage behind it.

When buying second-hand check that the construction is sound. Look underneath and inside cupboards and drawers to make sure nothing is warped and that there's no woodworm or other defect which will make the piece unusable. Warped drawers will not open, worm is expensive to cure and will spread to other things. Other items to look out for include shelves, mirrors, dressers or bits of dressers, hall furniture for coats and umbrellas and freestanding towel rails which are often made of wood and solidly built. Utility furniture, made to strict wartime specifications, can still be found. Such furniture was designed by some of the best manufacturers of the day so that, in spite of shortages of materials, decent furniture could be bought that was simple, well made and well proportioned.

Discount stores, swap shops and junk shops are all worth browsing in; local auctions, Salvation Army auctions and ex-government goods auctions are fascinating and can produce real bargains (look in local newspapers to see when and where they take place) and don't forget the humble jumble sale. Local newspapers, classified advertisements in magazines and local post office windows should not be ignored, and your municipal dump may have furniture too. Some dumps are so highly organized that you may have to pay for what you find there. Sometimes there is usable furniture sitting out in the street or in skips.

Don't forget to look in second-hand office furniture stores where typing chairs, desks, hat-racks and filing cabinets can all be turned into acceptable furniture in the right places.

It can be soothing and, ultimately, very satisfying to restore a piece of furniture to its former glory. There are many excellent stripping and sealing products available to give a professional finish.

Making a roller blind
*1   This is a basic roller blind kit,
plus a length of fabric and a can of
spray for stiffening it.*
*2   If you need to make seams in
your fabric, do ensure they're
symmetrical so the blind will roll
up evenly.*
*3   Turn up a hem deep enough
to thread the bottom batten
through.*
*4   Close the ends of the batten
opening with hand stitching.*
*5   With the spring mechanism
on the left, position the fabric
(right side up) straight along the
roller and tack into position. Don't
be tempted to substitute larger
tacks for the irritating little ones
provided in the kit. They are
purposely tiny so as not to
damage the mechanism.*
*6   Roll up the blind towards you
and fit into the brackets.*
*7   If the blind does not wind
smoothly, remove it from the
brackets and loosen it a little by
hand. Replace in the brackets.*

Few second-hand items will be exactly what you are hoping for and most will be very shabby, but a coat of paint and loose covers or new fabric stapled on can completely alter the look of the most unpromising object.

Using your ingenuity
There are many ways in which you can use your ingenuity in a Heath Robinson way while waiting for the right thing to turn up or the right money to get what you want.

If you can't afford trestles to support a table, use large boxes upended and covered with fabric. Or use a dustbin as a pedestal table base, spray it silver or some bright colour and cover it with a piece of laminated chipboard, cut to size, or piece of thick glass or a door.

Planks and bricks are the time-honoured materials for building cheap shelves. Use the idea with breeze blocks to build a low table.

Do-it-yourself blinds can be effective and cheap. All you need is fabric, a spray for stiffening it, the roller mechanism and a few tacks. You can buy DIY roller blind kits at many department stores and the fabric anywhere. If you can manage to do the spraying outside, so much the better because the spray smells awful. Choose a fine day and hang it out on a washing line if possible, or over the bath.

Foam blocks are often sold on market stalls. They can be cut to size and covered with cotton fabric to make seating or beds to fit awkward spaces.

Room dividers are a boon in small bedsits and can be as decorative as you like. Make your own screen as described on page 33.

A door can be used as a bed base, but you must drill holes in it so that the pints of water everyone sweats at night will have somewhere to evaporate.

Paint the floors with lino paint which you can get in all sorts of colours. It will make an enormous difference to the look of a room.

If you have an old travelling trunk or chest, cover it with foam rubber cut to fit the top. Glue it on and then cover the whole thing with fabric. This will make seating for one or two, and storage besides. Unaltered, it can make a base for the TV set or a plant.

Most aggressively ugly pieces of furniture can be made to fade into the background with a judicious coat of paint – or even come into their own as eye-catchers with really bright paint or stencils.

One fabric can unify a room which is full of ill-matched furniture. In fact, if you use the same basic colour you won't need to use the same design. Wallpapers and fabrics can often be bought which match or coordinate.

Make your own sitting or sleeping area by raising the floor with a wooden stage, or with planks on breeze blocks. Cover it with a couple of mattresses divided by a rug. Use the space underneath for drawers to store bedlinen, toys or shoes. A box in the middle will do as a table and one or two lights can be suspended above it or clipped to its sides.

Cover old dining-chairs by stapling fabric to them. Match with napkins, place mats or a tablecloth.

This room is a warren of narrow passages between boxes, suitcases and heaps of possessions. While the owner may enjoy the clutter, it is not very inviting or practical for visitors. Good storage and a mixture of low and high platforms could make it as welcoming as the room overleaf.

Lighting

Clever lighting can make most ordinary rooms look interesting, whereas inappropriate lighting can cut down efficiency, cause eyestrain, lead to accidents and, apart from all that, make a room very depressing to be in.

It is better, from the aesthetic point of view, to have lots of lights in different places than one high watt central light bulb. This may be difficult in a house with old wiring and not enough socket outlets, but you can solve that problem by buying a short extension lead attached to a small unit of three or four sockets. Several items which don't use up much electricity can be run off this.

Ideally, you will need three sorts of lighting:

1. *Task lighting* This is necessary for reading and working. It must be directed straight on to the page or work area without glaring into your eyes or casting shadows on the work.
2. *Background or ambient lighting* A wash of lights judiciously placed enable you to see the room and tell where you are going, without illuminating every corner with unnecessarily strong light.
3. *Highlighting* Certain objects, such as paintings or sculptures, and architectural features, such as arches or ceiling mouldings, can become points of greater interest when specially illuminated.

Harsh strip lighting does nothing to enhance this rather bleak room. Several small lamps (see overleaf), or even a central shaded light bulb, would make it a pleasanter environment.

Right: *This is a way of organizing one longish space into several distinct areas. The raised platform is carpeted throughout, the bead curtain helps to provide a sense of privacy and the discreet lighting helps to divide the separate areas too.*

Far right: *This picture shows a wide range of spotlamps and angled lamps available at very reasonable prices.*

Far right, centre: *Four versions of the cheapest and most effective way to hide a bare bulb hanging from the ceiling.*

Below: *Several table lamps placed round a room give a softer light than a single overhead light and need not be expensive to run if you use low-wattage bulbs.*

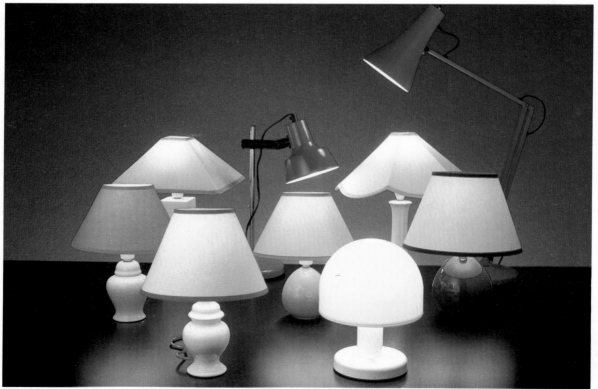

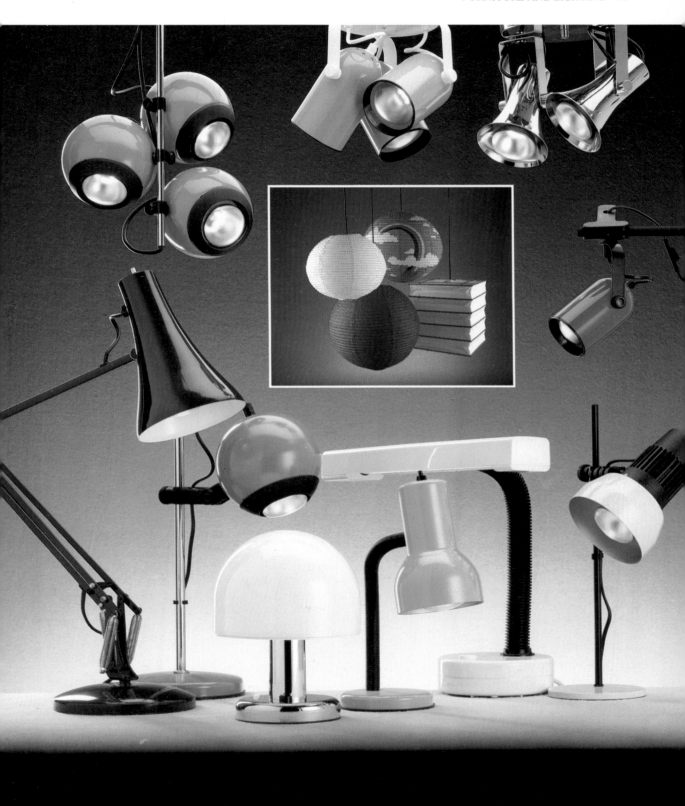

Working lights

Spotlights have been popular for some time now as useful working lights and as highlighters. One or two spotlamps over the cooker and kitchen worktops will help the cooking process. If you eat in the kitchen as well, you could have a 'rise-and-fall' lamp above the table. This can be pushed up out of the way or pulled down low for eating by. If you keep it low, you can turn the other kitchen lights off and you will be unaware of the cooking chaos all around.

Spotlights can be set into lighting track to create a row of directional light. You can normally get up to five spots in one piece of track, but you can also get joints so that it is possible to create, say, a square of track in the middle of the ceiling with the spots directed at different angles.

Track systems made by different manufacturers are not compatible and each will take only the lamps specifically designed for it. Shop around a little before deciding which you want.

Another excellent type of working light is the angled lamp, many variations of which can be found in most lighting shops or department stores. The great advantage of angled lamps is that they are portable and the light can be directed any way you please.

Background light

For really cosy lighting a good rule is to keep the lamps low to the floor. Blobs of light on the ground or on low tables give a delicate and pleasing result. Wall 'sconces' – lights with shades flat against the wall – make good ambient lighting which is subdued but efficient. Take care that wall or ceiling lights in passages, halls, corridors and stairwells won't cast shadows from the bannisters or anywhere else; this can be confusing and dangerous to the best of us, and more so to the very young and the very old.

Highlighting

Spots are good at highlighting paintings or arches, but you must take care that the light doesn't glare in other directions, making life uncomfortable for people. The bulb must always be concealed from view. You can get small tube lights on special mountings to illuminate pictures, but you may need to visit a specialist lighting shop to find them. Some stores sell small tube lights which are not specifically for pictures, but can be adapted for this purpose.

The advantage of having many low-watt lamps rather than one or two high-watt ones is that you can be flexible and alter the mood of a room easily. Three table lamps will give a good light for drinking and chatting; add a brighter light over a table and you can play games or sew; a single light over the table alone will provide a good ambience for an intimate dinner or for watching television.

Dimmer switches help to make lighting flexible and may even reduce electricity bills, though light bulbs don't consume much power anyway. In any case, dimmer switches are not expensive to buy and are particularly useful for children's rooms where you can turn the light right down without turning it off completely.

When placing your lighting, check that reflections in the television screen are not going to annoy you. You should be able to turn off strategic lights when you're viewing so that there are no reflections, but not have to sit in a completely darkened room.

In the bathroom, a light over the mirror will help for shaving and putting on cosmetics. Two small tubes either side of the mirror would do this job well. Rows of bulbs all round the mirror are a bit harsh on the eyes and the complexion – and ultimately, the confidence! If you have a full length mirror, direct the light so that you can see yourself properly in it.

Every bed should have a bedside lamp, and a double bed should have one on each side of a kind that can be angled so that one partner won't annoy the other by wanting to read in the middle of the night. Small children need a good overhead light for playing, but they need a bedside lamp as much as anyone else.

Although there are hundreds of different styles of lighting – spots, hanging lamps, wall lamps, table lamps, standard lamps, angled lamps, paper bag lamps, goose lamps, outside lamps, fluorescent lamps and low-wattage lamps – many of them are expensive and gimmicky and it isn't always easy to find something one really likes. However, good cheap lamps can be found in many chain stores.

When buying shades remember that colour, shape and material will all affect the amount and quality of light that gets through. A tubular shade will cast light over a small area while a pyramid-shaped one will have a much wider light path. Coloured cloth will let less light through than paper. Whatever the shade it should conceal the actual bulb. The reason those round Chinese lantern shades have been popular for so long is because, until recently, they were about the only shade which let most of the light through without glare, were pleasant objects in themselves, and made the best of the dreaded overhead light for people who couldn't afford other solutions. Unfortunately they have been used so much by so many people they've become rather clichéd. Recently, square and rectangular Japanese-style shades with coloured wooden frames have appeared on the market and opened up the possibilities.

In general, when buying shades it's better to plump for larger rather than smaller. Round globe lamps with pyramid shades always look better with large shades. Surprisingly you will find that the shade is often more expensive than the lamp, but covering a shade is cheap and easy; you can get the frames in needlework or craft shops and cover them with your own fabric. Cheaper still would be to recover an old frame.

Making your own lamps from bottles, jugs or figurines is easy and cheap, but the DIY fittings tend to be flimsy and don't last long in my experience. If you intend to make your own, buy the more solid-looking fittings from specialist shops as they tend to have a longer life than those found on market stalls.

Light bulbs

There are basically two different kinds of light bulbs for household use: incandescent bulbs, used for most domestic lighting, and fluorescent tubes, which give a strong white light and last longer for the same amount of power. Although very good for working, tubes tend to be rather harsh as general light. However, a warm white colour is now available and is gentler on the eyes.

When buying incandescent light bulbs take care to choose the right sort; some screw into the fitting and some have a bayonet fitting. With so many sizes to choose from do ensure that you will easily be able to find the size and type you need locally. It's sensible, though not always possible, to try and find lamps that take the same kind of bulb.

When buying a lamp check what bulb wattage it will take and don't put in a higher one. A perfectly good lamp can be melted or otherwise ruined by using too powerful a bulb.

An unattractive corner has been turned into a focus of interest by removing the top doors of the cupboard and installing concealed strip lighting to highlight the collection of corn dollies inside.

9 · Electrical and gas appliances

Equipment, by which is usually meant some sort of 'powered' contraption, such as a cooker or washing machine, is essential to the satisfactory running of a modern home. However, there are as many pieces of equipment about as there are daisies on a lawn and tempting though they may be, you will need hardly any of them. You'll want something to cook on, something for cold storage, a heater to keep the room warm and possibly a clothes dryer. Everything else is luxury and can wait until you have more money or more space.

Making a choice may prove difficult because a cooker may be anything from a giant solid fuel range with a double oven to a single electric ring which sits on the worktop. Equally, a fridge may be a five person monster with a large freezing section to cope with sides of beef and a winter's supply of oven-ready chips, or a table-top box big enough for a milk bottle and a carton of eggs. The general rule is the same as for furniture: if in doubt, don't get it. It's better to have too little than too much. If you can't find worktop space for a piece of equipment such as a blender, then you will find a place for it at the back of some cupboard, the pieces will be dispersed so it will be too much trouble to assemble and it will simply never get used.

What sort of fuel?

Should you choose gas or electricity? This is a question of personal choice in most homes. In rural areas the choice is between bottled gas rather than natural gas and electricity, but there's not really much difference to the user between the two types of gas, except that bottled gas has to be delivered and the cylinders changed at intervals. Gas may sometimes smell a little and some plants seem not to like it, but electricity is more likely to suffer from power failures.

Gas is measured by the therm and electricity by the unit. You can find out from your local electricity or gas showroom how much a unit costs at any particular time (it is not always exactly the same in different parts of the country) and they should be able to tell you the amount a particular type of equipment uses. For instance, 1000 watts of electricity used continuously for one hour equals one unit, so a 2000 watt fan heater run for one hour will have used two units.

Appliances these days are very much designed with energy saving in mind. This means that second-hand appliances though cheap to buy, may be rather more expensive to run than something bought new. Always look out for any energy-saving features in the equipment you are buying. Electric rings, for example, often have an inner section which you can heat up for small saucepans.

When buying second-hand equipment check that the lead and plug are in good condition and change them if they are frayed or scorched.

Space saving equipment

If you have only a small kitchen or a cooking area within another room, keep all your equipment to the barest minimum – not a pan or a plate more than you actually need. This may sound like counsel of gloom, but it's much pleasanter in reality than living with a whole heap of unidentifiable junk. Go round the shops and look for the smallest equipment you can see. Perhaps you should forgo the idea of a conventional cooker altogether. Even the smallest of these takes up a lot of space so measure carefully before buying. (Remember always to take your tape measure with you when shopping for the home.) On the whole cookers do seem to be unnecessarily bulky. Most have a grill at eye level and splashbacks which you might prefer not to have. All incorporate a large oven, and how often are you really going to want to use it? If you do want a 'proper' cooker, make sure it has a door which can be hung on the left or the right – crucial if space is very limited.

If you feel a large cooker is too wasteful of space, keep your eyes skinned for something rather different to the conventional cooker. Mini cookers are small enough to sit on a worktop and yet incorporate a small oven and two rings. You may be able to get a second-hand one in local auction at a good price, or you can buy a hob without an oven or a grill and fit it into the worktop. You can also buy single freestanding rings and with one of these, and a set of stacking saucepans or a pressure cooker, plus imagination and clever planning, you can produce a respectable meal without too much difficulty. Such a ring certainly saves space. A pressure cooker can also be extremely useful once you've discovered how to time things accurately.

Triple-purpose cookers are made which will do a variety of meals; they incorporate an oven, grill and rotisserie and will spit roast, grill or roast. You will have to study the instruction booklet with care until you have mastered all its subtleties. Some multi-purpose cookers are even more remarkable since they will stew, roast, bake, boil and steam food and double up as the pan as well as the cooker. These items are about the size of a large casserole and can be unplugged and placed on the table to serve from. What more could you ask?

There are several types of electric casserole available which cook very slowly and gently, emulating a pan in a very slow oven. They incorporate a good-looking piece of brown pottery with an electric element so they double up as the pan as well as the oven. Read the instructions carefully because you must get the food cooking properly before leaving it to simmer. This is an excellent way of simmering bones for stock, making stews, pot roasts, soups, rice puddings and even a Christmas pudding, when you don't want it cluttering up the cooker proper, should you have one.

Microwave ovens will do most cooking jobs, though they cannot brown a roast or make crackling on pork. They are good for thawing and heating up frozen food quickly, so are handy for those who get home late and hungry. They use less electricity than conventional cookers and are comparatively cheap to run.

A contact grill consists of two heavy aluminium ridged plates coated with non-stick material. Some will open right out providing twice the area for cooking on because you can use the lid as well. They are excellent for toasted sandwiches and can cope with steaks and sausages too.

Cookers tend to be functional objects rather than things of beauty so the simpler the design, the better. Remember too, that the fewer dainty chrome edges and moulded decorations it has, the easier it will be to clean, the less likely little bits will be to fall off and the better it will look in general.

Food storage

In winter you might get by without a refrigerator by keeping milk, butter and cheese on the windowsill or in the bathroom, until you want to eat them, though keeping things on the outside windowsill is not recommended in case something falls on to a person below. Anyway, in summer this is really not practicable and life without a fridge is frustrating and difficult. On the whole refrigerators seem to be fairly foolproof; there's not much to go wrong with them, although you may find that their interiors seem to be of rather poor quality plastic and likely to chip and crack.

Choose a small fridge (unless there are thirty-two of you living in a squat). There's no point in having a family-sized fridge if you are a single person with the appetite of a bird. Choose ones which have storage that you will find most convenient. For example, if you are passionate about ice-cream you will want a fridge with a large ice box; if it's yoghurt you're keen on, you'll need more fridge space than ice box.

However, if you just want somewhere to keep a couple of bottles and the butter cold, what you need is a refrigerator designed for campers, caravanners and people on boats. These are little box-shaped fridges with a couple of very narrow shelves and space in the door for eggs, milk and fruit juice. They run on gas or electricity and can usually be found in your local showrooms or camping shop. If you have difficulty finding such a fridge, look in camping, caravanning and boating magazines. If you have to sleep close to your kitchen area it's worth knowing that gas fridges are controlled by thermostat and there is no vibration so they are very quiet.

If you are a microwave cook there are equally tiny freezers

Kitchen equipment, such as this processor, may have many component parts. It is important to keep them together and accessible or you'll find it too much bother to assemble the equipment.

One of the most practical, best-looking and certainly the cheapest clothes horse: two sides of a drop-sided cot, slotted together to form an inverted V, has plenty of rungs to hang clothes on.

available which are perfectly adequate. They will hold up to 16 kg of frozen food and can sit on or under a worktop, or on top of a fridge.

Room heating

Central heating is undoubtedly the best for a large house, but may be either impractical or impossible financially for the small home dweller. However, efficient heating can be obtained by carefully choosing individual heaters, and needn't break the bank.

Electric fan heaters provide quick effective heating. The air blows the heat out into the room and can be directed high or low to warm the toes or the midriff. You'd probably need more than one in a large room. Fan heaters are said to be expensive to run, but because they are easy to regulate and switch on and off, you only use the amount of heat you need, so they are, in fact, quite economical, especially in small rooms.

Freestanding convector fires tend to be larger and squarer than fan heaters. The heat comes out of a grill at the top and can be regulated to adjust the amount of power you use.

Modern oil heaters are efficient and paraffin is a comparatively cheap fuel. They have several snags: you have to carry the fuel into the home; if not maintained properly the heaters will smell; they add to the moisture in the air, so if you suffer from condensation, it will get worse; in some cases they are banned because of the danger of fire. Many landlords ban them because their insurance policies say they must. Don't buy second-hand oil heaters or use them in homes where there are young children, and don't move them when they are alight. Provided you use paraffin heaters responsibly they can provide a comfortable and efficient form of heating.

Gas fires operate by a combination of radiation and convection and heat a room very quickly. They can maintain a comfortable temperature because the heat can be easily regulated.

Bottled gas heaters, although bulky are easy to regulate and highly effective. The main disadvantage is that the gas cylinder has to be refilled from time to time. These heaters, however, can efficiently heat large rooms, barn-like studios or warehouse conversions.

Bathroom· heating is difficult since the conducting properties of steam and condensation make electricity rather dangerous. The best answer is probably a combined light and radiant heater fitted to the ceiling. These can be adjusted to give light *or* heat, or light *and* heat together. They are operated by a pull switch at the bathroom door and warm up the space surprisingly quickly – in the time it takes to run a bath. Another useful source of heat is a long, slim infra-red heater fixed high on the wall, with its reflector angled to send the heat downwards.

Water heating

In a small flat, it may save space to have a wall-hung electric or gas heater rather than a tank with an immersion heater. Electric shower fittings use little electricity and water and take up much less space than a conventional bath. The heater itself, which sits on the wall next to the shower head, is neat and unobtrusive.

Gas water heaters provide hot water through a spout on the heater or through a shower or basin. Such heaters may be designed to boil water for a pot of tea or coffee, so take care nobody tries to wash their hands if you have one set to boiling temperature.

Clothes drying

Drying damp clothes can be a real nightmare in a place where there's no garden and very little space inside. Small tumble dryers are available and can additionally be used as a worktop in the kitchen, but you must be able to open the window or ventilate the room somehow. A new tumble dryer is now on the market, designed to collect the moisture in a condenser which you can empty out, but it's not cheap or particularly small.

A spin-dryer is probably more useful in a small space. Some are very neat and can be squeezed into a very cramped kitchen. If the spin-dryer is efficient it will eliminate enough water to make the clothes ready for ironing. You can spin woollen garments for a short time in this sort of dryer without damaging them and afterwards hang them up instead of laying them flat which saves much space and inconvenience.

Failing either of these pieces of electrical equipment, probably the most convenient form of dryer is a folding rack which fits over the bath. It is not particularly aesthetic, but it does keep damp clothes out of the way of ordinary living.

10 · Bringing your home to life

Most people don't feel really at home in their own house until they have stamped their personality on it in a very individual way. Of course, the colour of the paint, the arrangement of furniture and the choice of materials and equipment help to do this. But the final touches are like putting on your jewellery and make-up after you have got dressed. They can add futuristic glamour, Hollywood nostalgia or suburban cosiness, give your home a welcoming warmth and display certain aspects of your own personality which are vaguer in the general background of the home.

Paintings, posters and prints

Pictures of some sort are important accessories. Choose them because you like them, not because you think they will impress other people or be investments. If you follow your own tastes in this (as with everything else and as you almost certainly do with clothes) no matter how varied your choice, it will all fit with your personality and by some magic 'go' together.

If possible buy or acquire pictures unframed and choose the frames and the mounts yourself. There's something drearily anonymous about a houseful of pictures beautifully but identically framed in tasteful black and gold which takes no account of the nature of the pictures themselves. Some pictures look good in plain modern aluminium frames, others merit wide frames with large mounts, some look good with dark mounts, others are best with no mount at all. You can't really tell what will look best until you put the frames and the colours together.

One large painting or a poster can look good on a big wall, but if you don't possess such a thing, hang a series of identically framed pictures or a motley selection all together. And don't dismiss the kitchen, bathroom, bedrooms and hall as places to hang pictures of one sort or another.

Framed paintings, or sometimes frames on their own, can often be found in jumble sales or junk shops. You can discard the paintings and keep the frames for your own paintings or prints. If you don't strike it lucky at jumble sales, aluminium frames are simple to construct and you can get them from DIY shops in any size you like.

Above: *A wall of pictures with a connecting theme – in this case they are all family photographs. The very discreet pattern of the wallpaper does not detract from them.*

Left: *The haphazard placing of the pictures in this room does not show them to best advantage. It's a pity that the screen propped against the wall isn't used to hide some of the mess.*

Right: *An imaginative and practical way to use a simple white shelving system. Shelves of different widths provide storage for a wide variety of items, and the result is as decorative as it is useful.*

Alternatively, you can buy clip frames which are even easier and cheaper.

When hanging pictures think in terms of the wall rather than the picture. One small picture is liable to get lost unless it's something rather special which will hold its own. Single pictures (like single light bulbs in the ceiling) are often hung right in the middle of a wall where they may look lost and rather pathetic. If you hang your picture above a fireplace, or a chair next to an object or above a low table, or just on part of the wall which looks a bit blank, it will relate to its surroundings and not be so isolated.

Balance rather than symmetry is what you should try to achieve. Put pictures together to form a rectangle or a block. The very confident can ignore the rules and follow their instincts. If you don't feel too sure, other people's example will help to start you off. Look around and when you see something you really like, ask yourself what is so good about it and then consider whether something similar would not fit into your own scheme of things. Often room sets in department stores offer ideas, glossy magazines certainly do.

It's probably easier to hang paintings symmetrically but it may be more entertaining to hang them at random. It requires practice to get a good balance of large and small, dark and pale, heavy or light, but if you are prepared to play with them a bit, like doing a jigsaw puzzle, you'll eventually get a harmonious whole.

When it comes to hanging pictures you may be in some difficulty with the rules of your lease. Some landlords object to putty-type adhesive because it can tear the wallpaper when pictures are removed. Check first, or use drawing pins if in doubt. Framed pictures can sometimes be hung from a rail at the top of the wall. If there isn't one you might be able to fix a rail yourself. Failing that you could probably get away with hammering picture pins into the wall, provided you are prepared to wallpaper or otherwise cover them up when you leave.

Pictures need not be framed paintings or prints on paper at all. They can be directional signs, notices or anything visually interesting. A friend of mine collected small, round sweet tins and stuck them to the wall to make a colourful and changeable collage.

Postcards make fascinating, cheap and historical pictures. It doesn't take long to collect a fair number from people on holiday or those who correspond by postcard rather than by letter. If people don't send you ones you like, send one to yourself every time you go away. Pin them up on a cork board and you will soon have a complete wall collage. If you use cork tiles, make sure you get the thick ones sold as insulating cork, which are deep enough for a drawing pin to stick into. A frame round the cork will give it a more 'intended' and finished appearance.

Objects

One of the most difficult things in decorating is to store and show off objects to their best advantage, so that they don't take up space which you badly need for other things and don't look cluttered or untidy, but invite inspection and add to the charm of a room. These are the things that say the place is yours and displaying them can be highly rewarding. The secret is in the arranging. Five empty beer cans carelessly put down can look like the sleazy morning after a party, but the same number carefully built into a pyramid make a collection. Clutter is OK when it's intended and controlled, but when there are old shirt buttons and safety pins, and oddments of food lying among the arrangements the whole idea falls to pieces.

One trick is to line up objects carefully, have them facing the same way and in a carefully disciplined row, which creates immediate order from chaos. The same is true of books. If they are lined up with their spines along the edge of a shelf they will look neat and you will be able to find the title you want far more quickly than if they are all higgledy piggledy. From beach pebbles to wooden ladles, lace bobbins to biscuit tins and, of course, records and tapes – line them up in a disciplined order and they will become interesting objects instead of junk.

Collections of plates can also make a good wallful of interest and colour and they need not be Spode or commemorative. Many second-hand shops sell individual plates and a simple collection of perhaps white and blue can look very effective. Alternatively, plates picked up on holiday abroad can be a cheap way of achieving great style. I've seen such collections look splendid in bathrooms as well as kitchens, dining-rooms and living-rooms. Sometimes they take up a whole wall, sometimes they're simply a little cluster above a mantelpiece or in an alcove.

If you have a number of objects you are fond of but which you can't find space for, hang them from the ceiling. One young flat dweller I know has five mobiles (all from jumble sales or charity shops) and an inflatable duck hanging from her ceiling.

The bathroom is an excellent place for putting kitsch objects. Plastic flowers can brighten it up and a little 'bad taste' is just what that characterless little room needs to make going to the loo less of a penance. If you suffer from condensation, put in things that won't deteriorate because of the damp; metal might rust and fabric can go mouldy, so plastic is ideal.

Be prepared to change and shuffle things around from time to time, otherwise you get so used to them, you no longer see or appreciate the objects yourself.

Textiles

Colour, pattern and texture are the essence of a home and textiles play an important part here. In practical terms, woolly rugs and woven fabrics help to soften sound, but they also provide a solid comfort and warmth which make a place feel snug.

It is possible to provide splashes of sharp and brilliant colour through cushions and rugs which will liven up but not necessarily dominate the room. If you look carefully at different fabrics you will see how the softness and delicacy of silk contrasts with the rough warmth of wool; how the bold colours of a Portuguese rug

complement a plain coloured wall and how a delicate cotton print can add softness to an otherwise austere white bedroom.

Textiles above all else, repay time and patience in the choosing. They have to complement and enhance the rest of the room and must themselves look their best, without detracting from the other colours and patterns.

When choosing fabrics it's important to handle and touch them as well as to examine the colour in different lights. Tactile qualities are all important. There's an enormous choice and decisions are hard to make. In general though, a basic, simple peasanty room will benefit from primary and primitive colours and bold patterns; a modern angular room from bold bright geometric patterns and flat weaves and prints; a traditional English style from glazed chintz and pretty prints with gently patterned rugs or carpet.

Touches of colour

Interest in any colour scheme is achieved by contrast. The most tasteful or beautiful of colours will not be seen to best effect unless there is something opposite or contrasting to bring it to life. Even a bright red scheme will fail unless you can provide an opposite or contrasting colour, such as navy, to pull it all together and focus attention. Equally, if you opt for a pale and peaceful colour, you should provide touches of something bright and contrasting to

Opposite: This is a very carefully thought out and effective scheme, taking blue as its main theme. The plates and bottles were collected over a number of years. The willow pattern picture was painted by a friend.

accentuate its quietness. These patches of contrast need not be elaborate. In a kitchen, for example, one or two bright red or yellow mugs will do the trick and bring the whole scheme into focus.

Match up your colours carefully. Test them to see how they 'fit' together, and don't start off with any preconcieved notions about what goes with what; it depends on the room, the particular tone and strength of the colour involved, and on how large an expanse of it you want to have. It also depends on the texture, the lighting and on your own preferences and tastes. That old adage 'blue and green should never be seen' is ridiculous – though both the blue and green might benefit from a spot of contrasting red or black.

Colour can be provided by the bright red of a postcard on the noticeboard, by the colours in a poster, by the light shining through a particular lampshade, a painted picture frame, flowers, fruit or vegetables, a tablecloth, books – any number of things. Don't be afraid of contrast; it's the spice of life.

Mirrors

Mirrors are magic. They can practically double the amount of light you get in a room and give the illusion of twice as much space. The Arts Club in London has a mirrored wall which reflects the whole garden into the dining-room, giving a luxurious quality of space and elegance. If you are going to use mirrors, make sure they reflect something interesting or that they really do increase the light or make the room seem larger.

Mirror tiles can help to make a bathroom seem less poky, but less expensive is to buy a large sheet of mirror from a local glass merchant. It can either be screwed to the wall or you can put a frame round it. Beaded strips of wood are available at timber merchants and sometimes DIY shops. Second-hand mirrors are worth hunting for as new ones can be expensive.

11 · Plants

Plants are among the best pets you can have. They don't bite or scratch the furniture, they don't need feeding as often as animals and they don't need to be taken for walks. Provided they are healthy and flourishing, they provide colour and a real touch of life which adds something important to the most distinguished of interiors.

However, plants do need care and understanding. They grow best in the kind of atmosphere they originated from. Some ferns, for instance, need a lot more moisture than it is possible to provide in a centrally heated flat, while exotic plants, such as the velour philodendron require a hothouse and seldom receive the right treatment in the average home. A plant's natural habitat is a good guide to what sort of environment it will like – but there are many plants which flourish in the most unlikely circumstances and those are the ones to grow until you have gained a little confidence.

Plants need light, water and feeding during the growing season and the right temperature. In general, I suspect most people overwater their plants and since they need air as well as water, it is best with most plants, to wait until the soil on top is dry before watering again.

What to grow

Here are a few easy plants to start off with:

African violet (*Saintpaulia*) This is a small plant with fleshy, hairy leaves and purple or pink flowers which will flower all year round in a warm, sunny room. Plant several in a very large pot for an interesting display.

Aspidistra (*Aspidistra elatior*) A plant much grown by Victorians, it has strappy leaves and likes a cool atmosphere out of direct sunlight and a smallish pot.

Cacti (*Cactaceae*) These should be kept on sunny windowsills. Too little water will make them limp, but overwatering them will rot the base of the stem. Collections of cacti in a group usually look better than individuals.

Fig leaf palm or False castor oil plant (*Fatsia japonica*) This is very easy to look after. It has large glossy dark green leaves, but there is a variegated variety, tipped with creamy white. They like a fairly low temperature (about 50°F) in a light or lightly shaded part of the room, but not in direct sunlight. Keep the compost just moist during winter and in summer water fairly often.

Spider Plant (*Chlorophytum comosum*) This pretty plant is one of the easiest to grow and multiplies rapidly. It grows quickly, producing large numbers of arching, green and white striped leaves. It doesn't mind whether the room is warm or cool and likes bright light. Water frequently during summer. You can peg down the little plantlets into separate pots to make new plants.

Ivy (*Hedera*) This is an attractive plant that's easy to grow. There are many different types with innumerable permutations in the shapes and colours of their leaves.

Swiss cheese plant (*Monstera deliciosa*) If you want something large and imposing, this plant likes warmth and sun and will eventually need a large pot, a tall stake or two and plenty of space.

Poinsettia (*Euphorbia pulcherrima*) This has bright red bracts (modified leaves) which look like flowers. It likes a fairly high temperature and will give colour when everything else is dead or dormant.

Above: *Plants add life and colour to every room. Make a bold arrangement across a window to emphasize the plants and allow them to benefit from the light. Remember that few plants like direct sunlight so be careful in your choice.*

Opposite: *A refreshing way to put the television in its place: sit it on an old blanket chest, surround it with plants and a collection of prints and plates.*

Spiderwort (*Tradescantia*) This popular plant, also called 'Wandering Jew', 'Speedy Jenny' and 'Moses in the Bullrushes', is one of the easiest to grow. It likes light and a temperature no lower than 50°F. Water a lot in summer.

There are, of course, hundreds more plants to choose from, but the selection given here would make a good beginning. Bulbs can be planted before Christmas, kept in the dark (under a bed or the stairs) until the shoots are about two or three inches tall and then brought out to give pleasure when everything seems wintry and depressing.

How and where to use plants

You can use plants in many different ways and in many different places. Just remember that if you put a plant which needs warmth into a cold hall, it will die, and if you put one that needs bright light under the stairs, it too will die. Watch your plants for signs of distress, such as leaves dropping or losing colour, and try moving them to different places in your home.

Rows of plants can be used to divide up spaces in a large room. Trailing ivies can be trained to make quite an effective room divider. Hang plants from the ceiling where people will not knock their heads against them; near a skylight is ideal as it will provide the light they need. You must not forget to water them just because they are above your head.

Herbs are good plants for window boxes and windowsill pots since they look attractive and are useful too. Mint, sweet basil, thyme, parsley, chives and marjoram are particularly useful and easy to grow.

A low table near a window can be the basis for a miniature indoor garden, arranging plants with contrasting height, foliage and flowers.

Useful addresses

Advice sources

British Gas Showrooms Find the nearest branch in your local telephone book. Information on authorized gas dealers and installers; will supply manufacturers' addresses.

Building Centre, 26 Store Street, London WC1
Advice on manufacturers and materials, also on heating. Bookshop.

Citizens' Advice Bureaux Look in your local telephone book for the nearest office. Advice on consumer difficulties and rights.

Consumers' Association, 14 Buckingham Street, London WC2
Publishers of *Which?* magazine; will advise members on consumer problems.

Design Council, The Design Centre, 28 Haymarket, London SW1 and Design Council Scottish Committee, The Scottish Design Centre, 72 Vincent Street, Glasgow 2
Both have an ever changing series of exhibitions, an index of products chosen for their good design, a designer selection service, a bookshop, a 'good design' shop and a coffee shop.

Electricity Council, 30 Millbank, London SW1 P4RD
Advisory leaflets. You can find the address of the nearest showroom from your local telephone book.

Electrical Living Foundation (part of the Electrical Association for Women), 25 Foubert's Place, London W1V 2AL
Publications and classes. (You don't have to be a woman.)

Updating the old

Dylon International Consumer Advice Bureau, Worsley Bridge Road, London SE26
Will advise on dying: what kind of dye on what kind of fabric and when not to dye.

Renubath Services, 108 Fulham Palace Road, London W6 9PL
Bath repairing and resurfacing service; can deal with any enamelled baths.

Manufacturers and retailers

Astrohome Ltd, 47 Neal Street, London WC2
Packed with industrial and catering equipment for the home. Not always cheap but good for some items or getting ideas.

Bachers Fabrics, 58 High Street, Manchester M4 1DY
Huge range of dress materials, plus some furnishing fabric.

B & Q (Retail) Ltd, Head Office, Norwich House, Nelson Gate, Commercial Road, Southampton SO9 1RF
A chain of supercentres selling everything DIY for the home and garden, including carpets off the roll, bathrooms and kitchens. There are 150 branches spread throughout England, Scotland and Wales. They have some ranges of self-assembly furniture, mainly for kitchens.

British Home Stores, Head Office, 129 Marylebone Road, London NW1
This chain of stores is well known for its wide range of good quality merchandise at competitive prices, and in particular for its excellent lighting department.

Ceramic Tile Design, 56 Dawes Road, London SW6
A very wide selection of tiles. Other good sources for cheap tiles are Habitat, Laura Ashley and John Lewis.

Cubestore, 58 Pembroke Road, London W8
Has showrooms at Industrial Estate, London Road, Brandon, Suffolk and 47 Abbey Street, Nottingham. These shops design, manufacture and sell versatile modular storage systems, and wall-mounted and freestanding shelving systems. Catalogue available.

Estia Designs Ltd, 5 Tottenham Street, London W1
Sells foam furniture and has clever storage ideas.

Fix-n-Fit This is an offshoot of Fine Fare Supermarkets and has branches at Sutton in Ashfield, Hyde, Warrington, Castlegate, Grantham and Welwyn Garden City.
Run-of-the-mill decorating and home repair equipment, bedroom furniture and bedding, mainly of well-known brands such as Berger, Crown, Dulux, Schreiber and Carron. They have a rather useful line in single pine shelves, which can be used for decoration as well as storage.

G. Franchi & Sons, 331 Gray's Inn Road, London WC1
Sell metal brackets and pulleys for clothes airers.

The Futon Company, 10–12 Rivington Street, London EC2; 267 Archway Road, London N6; 654A Fulham Road, London SW6; 82–83 Tottenham Court Road, London W1
Manufacturers of traditional Japanese bedrolls and bases, and other Japanese inspired furniture.

Gratnells Ltd, 256 Church Road, Leyton, London E10 7JQ
Manufacture and sell a plastic-coated wire system for organizing storage within cupboards, drawers and shelves.

Habitat, Head Office, Hithercroft Road, Wallingford, Oxon
Chain of stores selling good design at reasonable prices. Excellent for kelim rugs, fabrics, kitchen and dining equipment and all sorts of bright, well designed items for the home.

John Lewis Partnership, Oxford Street, London W1
A chain of shops with the slogan 'never knowingly undersold', which sells good quality furniture, lighting, wallpaper, paint, tiles, rugs, carpets and most things for the home.

Laura Ashley, Decorator Collection Showroom, 71 Lower Sloane Street, London SW1 and Mail Order Department, Box 1, Laura Ashley Ltd, Carno, Powys, Mid Wales
Branches throughout the country sell this basically English floral collection of paints, matching fabrics and wallpaper at very good prices.

Lyn le Grice Stencil Design, St Buryan, Cornwall TR19 6HG
Small and large stencil kits for chests of drawers, floors, doors, freezers, fridges and so on. Catalogue available.

MFI Furniture Centres Look in the telephone directory for your nearest branch. A chain of supercentres selling self-assembly furniture, kitchen and plumbing equipment.

Northern Cork Supplies, 53 Rooley Moor Road, Rochdale, Lancs OL12 7AX
Cork floor and wall tile specialists. Full colour catalogue including samples of some wallcoverings. Seconds may be available.

Oxfam Trading, Murdock Road, Bicester, Oxon OX6 7RF
Mail order catalogue. Baskets, Numdah rugs, dhurries and bedspreads produced by cooperatives in developing countries. You can't always get these things in Oxfam shops.

Reject Tile Shop, 178 Wandsworth Bridge Road, London SW6
Sells ends of lines: some may have slight variation in glaze or tone but no broken, cracked, damaged or substandard tiles.

Russell & Chapple, 23 Monmouth Street, London WC2 H9D
Sell hessian, polythene sheeting, piping and pvc-coated fabrics at trade prices. They are wholesalers who will sell to the public but you should be prepared to buy several yards and know what you want. They have no time for people who fuss around.

Storemore, 153 High Town Road, Luton, Bedfordshire
Small showroom showing their wire racks and baskets for making the most of cupboard space. Open Monday to Friday, 9.00 to 3.30.

Tile Traders Ltd, 16b St Paul's Place, off St Paul's Road, Islington, London N1
Sells imported ceramic tiles at what they call 'back of lorry' prices. They bulk buy perfect Italian tiles and sell from their warehouse.

Miscellaneous

Architectural Salvage, Hutton and Rostron, Netley House, Gomshall, Surrey
Second-hand building materials. Will supply lists of items in stock.

Arrowtip Plastics, 31–35 Stannary Street, London SE11
Manufacture and retail polystyrene granules for making sag bags.

Hire Service Shops, Head Office, Warenne House, 31 London Road, Reigate, Surrey
A countrywide organization hiring out equipment for building, decorating, gardening, cleaning, etc. Find your nearest branch in the local telephone directory. Many towns have their own individual hire shops where you can get sanders, drills and almost anything else you might need.

Frank Bowen, 15 Greek Street, London W1
Fortnightly auctions of office furniture. Many towns have their own auctions; look in your local paper for information.

The London Architectural Salvage and Supply Company, Mark Street, EC2 4ER
Second-hand taps, shower screens, towel rails, basins, lavatory seats and other basic equipment.

Walcot Reclamation, 108 Walcot Street, Bath BA1 5BG
Buys, swaps and sells most articles concerned with buildings except furniture: timber roofing materials, doors, arches, taps and sinks.

Wallpaper Warehouses, 105 Church Street, London NW8; 32 Willesden Lane, London NW6; 46–48 Willesden Lane, NW6; 142–144 Kenton Road, Harrow; 714–722 London Road, Hounslow, Middlesex
Sell wallpaper by well-known manufacturers at discount prices.

Bibliography

There are lots of books available that dump owners might find useful. Here is a selection.

COLLINS DO-IT-YOURSELF ENCYCLOPAEDIA (Salamander Press, 1976)
THE COMPLETE DECORATING BOOK by Corinne Benicka (Hamlyn, 1980)
THE DECORATING BOOK by Mary Gilliatt (Michael Joseph, 1981)
THE HOUSE STYLE BOOK edited by Deyan Sudjic (Mitchell Beazley, 1984)
HOW TO BUY SECOND-HAND by Richard Ball (Astragal Books, 1981)
ONE ROOM LIVING by Sue Rowlands (Design Council, 1977)
SETTING UP HOME by Nicholas Hills and Barty Phillips (Design Council, 1978)
THE WHOLE HOUSE OMNIBUS by Richard Ball (Astragal Books, 1978)

Index